Best wishes to Michael in hopes this will inspire you to great heights —

Ross Pennie

March 15/2008

The
Unforgiving
Tides

A young doctor encounters mud, medicine and magic on a remote South Pacific island

Ross Pennie

Manor House Publishing Inc.

Archives of Canada
National Library of Canada
Cataloguing in Publication Data:

Pennie, Ross A., 1952-

The Unforgiving Tides :
The true story of a young doctor's encounters with mud, medicine
and magic on a remote South Pacific island / Ross Pennie

ISBN 0-9736477-0-1

1. Pennie, Ross A.
2. CUSO - Biography
3. Physicians - Papua New Guinea - Biography
4. Physicians - Canada - Biography
5. Volunteers - Papua New Guinea - Biography
6. Volunteeers - Canada - Biography
7. Papua New Guinea - Biography. I. Title.

R464.P485A3 2004   610' 92
C2004-905662-X

The publisher gratefully acknowledges the financial support
of the Book Publishing Industry Development Program
(BPIDP) under the Department of Canadian Heritage.

Acknowledgements

This book has smouldered within me for decades.

It took a number of writing mentors to teach me the skills and give me the confidence to set it alight, among them Mark Frutkin, Martin Kendrick, Phyllis Theroux, Ray Robertson, Shyam Selvadurai, and Brian Henry.

Week after week, my writing buddies in Hamilton gave me the energy and feedback to weed out the worst of its flaws.

My heartfelt thanks go to John Bandler, Ron Deans, Shirley Edwards, Birgit Elston, John Hewson, Bob Love, Patricia McMullen, Maureen O'Connor, John Passfield, and Rickie Pattenden.

Michael B. Davie, my editor and publisher, brought this book to life with more expertise and enthusiasm than I could ever have expected or imagined.

Most of all, I thank my wife Lorna, my sister Sheena, and my parents, Barbara and Archie, for their unfailing faith in my instincts and abilities.

Disclaimer

The events related in this work of creative non-fiction took place essentially, but not exactly, as described.

The island of New Britain, Catholic Mission Vunapope, the hamlet of Kokopo, and the town of Rabaul are portrayed as accurately as the writer's memory permitted, but the characters' names and identifying details have been altered to protect their privacy.

The spelling of the New Guinea Pidgin passages has been modified to make them more comprehensible to the reader.

Advance praise for *The Unforgiving Tides:*

From the opening pages, readers will be immediately engaged by Pennie's evocative prose and find themselves immersed in a compelling story that goes straight to the heart.

A born storyteller, Pennie deftly transports the reader to the South Pacific where the young doctor receives a harsh initiation into the world of medicine.

In Papua New Guinea, Pennie encounters magic – and so will Pennie's readers.

Cathy Vasas-Brown, author, *Every Wickedness, Some Reason in Madness*

An honest, compelling tale of life, death, and the mystery of all that lies in between.

Ray Robertson, author, *Moody Food* and *Mental Hygiene: Essays on Writers and Writing*

…an obvious gift for storytelling… warm and engaging.

Angelika Glover, Editorial Assistant, Alfred A. Knopf Canada.

…imaginative and captivating… engaging… reminiscent of James Herriot – except Pennie examines the most intriguing creatures of all: fellow humans on a remote and exotic island.

Michael B. Davie, publisher, author, *Why Everybody Hates Toronto*

This is powerful writing that is at times deeply touching.

Brian Henry, Ryerson University

The Unforgiving Tides

Dedication

This book is dedicated to the thousands of CUSO volunteers who have ventured to the far corners of the world to make a difference, person-to-person, day-by-day.

Manor House Publishing Inc.
www.manor-house.biz   905-648-2193

Foreword

Ross Pennie has a story to tell.

And tell it he does in an imaginative and captivating manner.

Pennie's unassuming manner hides life experiences many of us can only dream about: As a young doctor, he provided health care – and in many cases life-saving operations - to the inhabitants of a primitive South Pacific society.

As a CUSO volunteer, the young doctor laboured in oppressive heat and could eat little, his dramatic weight loss mute testimony to his willingness to compromise his own health to help others.

Papua New Guinea was a very young nation when Pennie arrived, fresh from a Canadian medical school.

Eager to make a meaningful difference, Pennie contended with mud, tribal/bush medicine and magic. He removed a gigantic cyst from one women, delivered the babies of others, concocted remedies to counter exotic poisons, and overcame his own crisis of confidence.

Fascinating material. But can he write?

In a word, yes.

Ross Pennie is a cool, refreshing breeze sweeping a literary landscape cluttered with overwrought egos and self-serving scribes.

Pennie is a modest, yet exceptionally talented writer who cares a great deal about communicating clearly with the reader – qualities often in short supply.

As publisher of this book and author of more than a dozen of my own, I can attest to the constant challenge of having to never lose sight of the reader's interest. No matter how much a subject may be of interest to the writer, the telling of the tale must engage the reader or the book has failed to achieve its primary purpose.

Pennie never loses sight of this objective.

This is engaging prose, reminiscent of James Herriot – except Pennie examines the most intriguing creatures of all: fellow humans on a remote and exotic island.

Pennie takes us into this little-known world with engaging prose and touching, insightful passages.

Along the way, we meet a fascinating array of characters and feel as if we truly know them, such is Pennie's skill at conveying the colourful personalities of the Papua New Guineans, Canadians, Americans, Australians and transplanted German nuns who inhabit the pages of this very well-written book.

Readers everywhere will also come to sympathize with Pennie's trials and tribulations as he turns to ingenuity and untried remedies to counter a lack of experience and lack of medical supplies. And readers will embrace many other aspects of Pennie's learning experiences on a brutally hot Papua New Guinea island.

But Pennie has given us far more than an entertaining visit to an exotic locale. This is a journey into the private world of patient and doctor, of faith and trust, of life and death.

The two-year CUSO posting was clearly a time of great pressure and high expectations. Readers are certain to sympathize with Pennie as he contends with an inhuman workload, unfair assumptions and morale-destroying indifference to his efforts.

Pennie brings us an adventure that few among us will ever experience.

What's also apparent is that this was a soul-searching, coming-of-age period in Pennie's life.

It was then, in the shadows of jungle-choked volcanoes, that the young doctor interacted in a myriad of professional and personal relationships, felt exuberance, succumbed to grief, encountered cultural differences, questioned his existence, and experienced the reality of what it means to practice medicine when lives hang in the balance.

With skillful touches of humour and insight, Pennie brings us a collection of gripping adventure stories, rich in emotional detail, that will have you eagerly turning page after page.

I can't remember the last time I so thoroughly enjoyed reading a book, any book, even one of my own.

- **Michael B. Davie,** *The Unforgiving Tides* publisher, and the author of *Why Everybody Hates Toronto*

About the Author

Born in 1952, Ross Pennie spent his early childhood on the prairies of Southern Alberta and attended high school in the shadow of the Peace Tower in Canada's Capital, Ottawa.

Charged by the writings of R.M. Ballantyne, Daniel Defoe, Henry Morton Stanley, Robert Louis Stevenson, Thor Heyerdahl, and Jules Verne, he brought to medical school a long-nurtured desire to practise overseas in a remote setting.

On the completion of his MD at Queen's University, Kingston in 1976 and his twelve-month internship at Victoria Hospital, London, Ontario, he embarked on his two-year adventure with CUSO in Papua New Guinea.

After his South Pacific experience, filled to the brim with sick children and tropical micro-organisms, he completed training in the specialties of Pediatrics and Infectious Diseases.

He then worked as a medical practitioner, educator, and researcher at hospitals and universities in Canada, USA, St. Lucia, Brazil, and Malaysia.

Dr. Pennie is currently a professor at McMaster University, Hamilton and a practising physician at Brant Community Health System at Brantford, Ontario.

He's also a specialist in the treatment of infectious diseases.

Dr. Pennie resides in Hamilton where he shares his love of adventure travel with his wife and their two children.

Contents

Prologue

In 1977, I was a year out of medical school, barely finished my internship, and convinced I could pull magic out of a doctor's bag.

I volunteered for a two-year stint with CUSO at a Catholic mission on a remote South Pacific island, where an array of tribes practised bush medicine and magic in the sweltering heat.

It was an uneventful stay, except... I faced amputating a young woman's leg with a handsaw; I performed my first-ever appendectomy during an earthquake; the hospital was turned into a temporary tavern to treat alcohol poisoning victims with free drinks; I delivered babies unassisted; I broke a baby's collar bone to free her from the mother's birth canal; I removed a woman's giant cyst, bigger than any baby; I travelled deep into the jungle to find the source – a fertility elixir – and cure for an outbreak of typhoid fever; I treated a well-endowed Australian's sexually transmitted diseases; I developed a therapeutic milk formula that saved the lives of scores of malnourished children; I grappled with culture shock and indifference to my efforts; and I encountered a life-altering crisis of confidence that left me questioning why I'd ever gone to Papua New Guinea in the first place.

Along the way, I contended with cantankerous hospital staff and an island full of colourful characters. I also learned many valuable life lessons, and these too are shared in the pages of this book. This is my story. And I'm sticking to it.

- **Ross Pennie**

1

Dokta?

A jarring ring! Shaken, I slid a hand across sweat-soaked sheets, fumbling for the phone in the brutally hot night air. I grabbed the receiver on the second ring.

A female whisper barely rose above the crackles on the line. "Dokta?"

"Yes, it's Doctor Pennie," I rasped, reluctantly shaking the last blissful shreds of a rare, deep sleep.

"This is Children's Ward."

"Yes," I said impatiently. The phone line connected me to the mission's hospital, a short jog from my own quarters at Catholic Mission Vunapope, neighbouring the hamlet of Kokopo in northeast Papua New Guinea.

"Wanpela pikinini meri i-come, i-got pekpek wara," the nurse stated in a Pidgin, advising me a girl has severe diarrhea.

Now the voice switched back to English: "And Dokta," she added, "we can't find the blood pressure. Sorry, Dokta."

A pause, then: "You coming now, Dokta?"

No detectable blood pressure – the child must be in shock. There was no point asking for more details. "Yeah," I sighed. "I'll be there right away."

I sprang out of bed, knocking my paperback to the floor. I'd read three such potboilers in the six days since I arrived at Vunapope mission. There was little other entertainment available in this primitive outpost in the South Pacific two thousand miles away from any place I'd ever learned about in school.

The entire sun-baked collection of islands north of Australia had just one radio station and no television. What passed as a cinema in Papua New Guinea was a smoke-filled hall with a torn screen and a temperamental projector. These rough-hewn filmhouses served up a menu of Kung-fu movies and ancient Hollywood westerns.

Snaking out of the mission, past the hamlet of Kokopo, and along the coconut coast was a rough strip of tarmac that terminated in the lazy, heat-shimmering avenues of Rabaul. A car could make the trip in under an hour if the radiator didn't run dry halfway there. The town was home to fifteen thousand humans, as many barking dogs, and four jungle-green volcanoes that coughed and shuddered in their sleep. Two main streets boasted clapboard businesses – banks, department stores, hotels, Chinese restaurants. Like the road, the phone line from my house stretched no further than Rabaul.

I had found myself in Papua New Guinea – PNG – as a result of my own lobbying. While in medical school in Canada, I had eagerly volunteered to serve on an overseas assignment with CUSO (the initials once meant Canadian University Service Overseas but the acronym had become a name unto itself).

Fresh out of medical school, I headed for PNG to practice medicine among people who just as frequently turned to spirits and magic to heal them. My posting was in New Britain, an island off PNG's northeast coast.

I threw a clean shirt over my twenty-five year-old frame, slid my feet into flip-flops, grabbed my army-surplus canvas satchel, and ran through the door – all in one continuous motion.

My year of interning at a big London, Ontario hospital, just a few weeks behind me, hadn't made me a seasoned medical practitioner. But it had taught me how to hustle. A three-minute dash took me up the driveway, across the dewy lawn, and into the children's ward.

12

The paediatric bungalow looked and felt more like a rustic kitchen than a hospital. Waist-high counters, with cupboards above, lined two walls. Although the place was tidy, dim lighting and faded paint made it appear grimy.

Swells of air – heavy with the odours of sweat, grease, and cabbage – oozed over me like warm molasses. My chest heaved from the jog up the hill.

At the far end of the room, beside an iron trolley table, a chunky teenager stood rolling strips of white cotton into bandages. She had nutmeg skin and wore the navy shift and white apron of a student nurse.

Near her, a clove-skinned nurse shook pills from a bottle and counted them onto a tray.

Now, a third student approached as the door swung shut behind me. Taller than the others, she had cinnamon skin, five chevrons tattooed unevenly across her forehead, and a wide halo of shimmering black hair, almost too springy to support her cap. Pinned to her apron was a nametag stating: "Veronika."

This late at night, the supervising nuns were asleep in their beds. Now it was just the three student nurses – all of them teenagers – joining me, an untested doctor in his mid-twenties.

Veronika looked straight into my eyes. "Good evening, Dokta. I'm sorry I disturbed you. But – but the girl is very sick."

In the centre of the room a little girl, about three-years-old, lay naked on a grey table. Her eyes were closed. A cowrie shell, dangling from a fibrous thread around her neck, rose and fell with the rhythm of her bird-like chest.

A stocky, barefoot couple, presumably her parents, crouched together in a corner, their eyes fixed on the table. Dry mud splattered their limbs. Their chests were bare, and each wore nothing but a *laplap* – a crude skirt fashioned of red and black cotton wrapped around the waist like a flimsy bath towel. Crops of open sores, raw and crusty, oozed from their earth-brown skin.

"What's her name?" I asked.

Veronika lifted a clipboard chart from the counter and scanned its front sheet. "Lillianna, Dokta."

I pulled my stethoscope from my satchel and bent over the child, listening with one ear while Veronika gave me the story. For the past few days, Lillianna had severe *pekpek wara* – watery poop.

Tonight, when she became too weak to sit up, the family made the trek from their village to the hospital.

The girl's unresponsive state had alarmed the nurses into calling me, especially when they couldn't detect her blood pressure.

My fingertips gently touched her forehead. Lillianna's skin had the feel of crinkled brown paper.

Her cheekbones bulged grotesquely; her dark eyes lay sunken and unfocussed in their sockets; her mouth gaped in a prolonged but silent scream.

Because her vital body fluids, lost in countless liquid stools, had not been replaced, she had withered like a houseplant deprived of water – a desiccated violet with a faint pulse and no flicker of consciousness.

Having descended into shock, she would suffer a cardiac arrest at any moment unless I could deliver a salvo of fluids into her bloodstream.

I quickly barked orders, and the nurses, in search of supplies, scattered like startled pigeons towards drawers and cupboards.

When the student nurses couldn't produce the swab, the needle, the salt solution I wanted instantly, a heavy knot of panic gripped my stomach and rose into my throat.

"Don't just stand there, get that I.V. bottle ready." My words echoed loudly and their harshness surprised me; but I couldn't stop the explosive volley. "I want it now, not tomorrow. For heaven's sakes hurry up!"

Jabbing at one site after another on the child's hands, wrists, and forearms, I shot for a vein, any vein, which would accept a needle. But they all had collapsed from dehydration.

I despaired of ever getting the intravenous running.

In one final try, I tightened the rubber tourniquet high on Lillianna's arm, felt for a vein at the elbow with as much care as my agitated state would permit, and stabbed at something vaguely like a vessel. There was a flash of blood. The needle had hit a vein!

I secured the intravenous tubing, opened the valve wide, and let the infusion run full speed.

The colourless solution left the bottle in a barrage of hurried droplets.

Within minutes, one quarter of the bottle's contents had poured into her bloodstream.

Veronika held Lillianna's wrist and calmly reported that the girl's pulse felt a little stronger. A few minutes later, the pulse was stronger still.

One of the nurses had pumped up the blood pressure cuff and actually managed to get a reading. We had now reversed the girl's shock—we were winning.

The odds of a cardiac arrest were dwindling to nothing. Lillianna even looked better. The corpse-like pallor of her lips had given way to a hint of colour.

I took a deep, calming breath.

Then, inexplicably, the little girl's eyes rolled upwards.

Her arms and legs stiffened like the branches of a Canadian poplar in winter. Her lips leered a gargoyle's grimace across clenching teeth.

For a minute, maybe more, she lay motionless on the table—a piece of driftwood, dry and contorted.

Her breathing ceased. A sickly blue tarnished her lips and gums. Green spittle welled from her slackened mouth.

The pulse in her neck grew weaker and slower until every muscle in her body slumped in a single, soundless sigh.

I listened for a faint heartbeat, desperate to hear at least a flutter. Nothing.

"She's arrested!" I shouted, the stethoscope still plugging my ears. "We have to do CPR. Can any of you give mouth-to-mouth?"

No answer came from the three teenagers at my side.

Two of them looked expectantly towards Veronika; she raised her eyebrows a fraction, wrinkling the tattooed chevrons on her forehead. Yes, she could do it.

"All right," I said urgently, "you start the mouth-to-mouth. I'll do the cardiac massage."

With steady hands, Veronika lifted the toddler's chin, pinched the nose, and blew into the reluctant lungs.

Then, with crossed hands, I pumped up and down on the breastbone.

I called for injections – adrenaline, bicarbonate, calcium. The minutes ticked by.

"Can you feel a pulse?" I asked. My voice was hoarse, strained with despair.

"No, Dokta."

"More adrenaline. Hurry!"

The parents cowered against the wall. Their faces gaped in horror. Desperation – theirs and mine – threatened to consume me, but I dared not break the rhythm of my slippery palms against the small chest.

After twenty minutes there still was no heartbeat. The inner candle of life had guttered and burned out; no amount of shouting, injecting, inflating, and pounding could re-light its flame. Lillianna, alive only minutes ago, was now deceased.

I gave the signal to stop with a waving motion of my heavy, down-turned palms. We took our hands off the body and stood transfixed in a ring around the table.

Moments later there began a heart-rending wailing, a screeching of startling intensity. In a wild delirium, the parents rocked their heads and flung their arms. They moaned and staggered and pawed and clutched – at each other, at me, at their flaccid child upon the table.

I forced myself to not recoil at the strong smells of fermented sweat, smoke, and feces rising from the grime on their unwashed bodies.

With our resuscitative efforts terminated, I didn't know what to do next. A minute ago, I had been the dominant force in the room. Now, I felt out of place, a stranger.

I backed away from the table, leaned heavily against a counter, and stared at the patterns made by the cracks in the concrete floor.

The mother sobbed her little girl's name over and over, stroking her cheeks with an unbearable tenderness.

A wave of nausea rose from deep within my belly and swept hard into my throat. I needed to leave. Now. I grabbed my satchel to escape into the moonless night.

I bolted from the hospital and headed down the driveway towards the rhythmic sound of the sea crashing against the reef. The wind hissed through the coconut fronds high above me. In the distance, two dogs barked a duet of warning and fear.

The avenue soon led me to the main coastal road, my flashlight's beam barely revealing the potholes in the crumbling asphalt.

I crossed the roadway, carefully edged my feet down the grassy embankment, and stepped onto the beach.

In a spot above the high tide mark I found a log, which long ago had been hauled up like a lost whale. The broken shells of hundreds of dead barnacles covered its sides, but its top was smooth, polished by years of sea spray, wind, and rain.

I sat down in a saddle-shaped groove between two knots and let out a long sigh that was lost in the sound of crashing waves.

Sharp scents of iodine and dead fish wafted upwards from the dry beach sand beneath my toes. The unseen rollers, bursting one after another onto the outer reef, boomed a hypnotic chant.

After some time, I rose and gathered a handful of smooth, flat stones. Heeding a summertime compulsion imprinted during my childhood in the Gatineau Hills of Quebec, I skipped them one by one across the surface of the water. The stones went click, click, plop as they skimmed the gentle swells of the lagoon.

For a moment, I was a carefree boy standing on a Canadian lakeshore on the other side of the world, sunshine blazing my cheeks, and the smell of pine needles tickling my nostrils.

The clock atop Saint Mary's Church clanged, wrenching me back to New Guinea time and the reality of my CUSO mission.

As a sliver of moon crept out of the sea, the mission buildings emerged from the void.

The angular shapes of the wharves and warehouses on the foreshore blocked most of the view of the church beyond them, but I could see the steeple's luminous cross of white neon.

Alone and miserable, I returned my attention to the shoreline.

I flicked one last pebble into the water. My footprints in the sand were the only other indication of a human presence.

Turning away from the breakers, I began trudging inland.

But with a backward glance I witnessed the warm water rush in toward my footprints, the tides playfully licking the tips of my toeprints, but otherwise leaving my tracks intact.

The next wash of warm salty water fell short of the footprints, seemingly content to let them be and accept this modest alteration to the raw beachscape. But with another surge, the tides consumed them, removing any trace of my presence in a slick of wet sand.

The brief impression I'd made was now erased, lost in the unforgiving tides. It was as though I was never there.

With a sinking feeling in my stomach, I wondered if this was also prophetic of my voluntary posting.

Was I to endure further medical failures, fall short of the CUSO goal of fostering lasting positive change and in the end leave only a soon-forgotten impression?

I pushed these haunting questions from my mind. If I intended to survive the next two years here at Vunapope Mission, I would have to focus purely on the tasks at hand, confront my failures and learn from them.

I headed back to the children's ward. Outside the entrance to the ward, a heavy-set man leaned against a pickup truck.

He drew on a cigarette and greeted me with a nod. *"Goodnight, Dokta. Me kam kisim pikinini belong wantok belong me."* He'd come to collect his neighbour's child.

I nodded in response.

He shook his head slowly. *"Sorry tumas."*

"Yes," I agreed. "Sorry too much."

He took a last puff and dropped the butt onto the dirt, then shrugged and ground the embers with his heel.

I pulled open the hospital door and braced myself for the misery of the unbroken keening.

But the room was silent.

The nurses were back to rolling bandages and counting pills. The grieving parents were caressing their child's skin with a moist cloth, rubbing the spatters of blood from her arms where I'd made so many stabs with my needle. Her limbs and buttocks were thin and wasted, as if she'd been deprived of food for weeks, even months.

The father wiped green spittle from Lillianna's chin and plucked bits of green-grey seeds from her kinky hair. I hadn't noticed the strange-looking seeds before. They looked like broken pieces of velvet-covered buttons.

The mother reached into a string bag and pulled out a length of cotton, printed in blue flowers.

Although the material was smudged with grime and ripped along one edge, she spread it on the table and flattened the wrinkles as best she could.

She helped her husband lift the little girl onto the impromptu shroud and fold it over her, leaving her face for us all to see.

The father, his pectorals broad and bulging, picked up his daughter to cradle her in his arms as though carrying her off to bed.

"Tenkyu, Dokta." His face held no hint of anger or resentment. Just resignation.

"Bai mipela i-go long place wantime Lillianna," he said as he pushed open the door with his shoulder. They were ready to take Lillianna home.

Before following them out the door, the mother dropped her bag and grasped my hand with both of hers. Her hands were sweaty and leathery against my skin, but warm and solid. She gave a squeeze. *"Tenkyu, Dokta. Tenkyu tru."*

I swallowed hard and barely managed to nod in reply.

The doors creaked and banged as the couple settled into the truck. The engine revved, the gears grumbled, and the vehicle rattled into the night.

There would be no formalities to mark Lillianna's death. No undertaker, no autopsy, not even a death certificate. Just a simple grave in the family garden between the taro and banana plants.

I picked up several pieces of seed that had fallen onto the floor.

They felt smooth and soft, like satin or velvet. "Do you girls know what these are?"

No answer. Just stony faces.

"Come on, girls," I insisted. "Tell me what they're for."

Still no answer.

"*Please,*" I implored impatiently. "You can tell me."

"Bush medicine," one of them whispered.

"Hush," hissed Veronika. "Matron says we're not to talk about it – says it's poison."

"Poison! Are they really poisonous?" I asked.

Veronika's shoulders stiffened. "We don't believe in that stuff." She lifted my satchel off the counter, handed it to me, and shot me a look that warned they'd said too much already. I got the message: It was time I went home.

In the guava trees beside my garden gate, the fruit bats screeched and chattered above me in the darkness. I couldn't tell whether they were fighting, playing, or warning of my approach.

My heart, too, was a jumble: there was blinding disappointment, but with it a feeling of hope, of inner release.

Perhaps the bush medicine, not my ineptitude, had provoked Lillianna's fatal seizure. I fingered the seeds I'd secreted in my pocket and reflected on how I might achieve my CUSO mandate of affecting lasting positive change in a primitive culture where poison can be embraced as medicine, where death comes too often to the very young, where few people live long enough to celebrate their fiftieth birthday.

Abruptly, a sound trilled louder than the squeals in the guavas. The telephone, its ring jarring and insistent, summoned through the open louvers of my unlit bedroom window. I fumbled for my house key, shoved open the door, and hustled to answer what was sure to be another emergency call.

2

Michael Toliman

I awoke the next morning to the staccato clucking of a hen scolding her chicks, warning them of the dangers of straying too far into the flowerbeds beneath my open window.

Through a crack between the curtains, a white-hot sabre of sunlight struck me in the eyes.

My bedroom was already a blast furnace. The day's delicious first hour after dawn – when the sun is still low and the air has a tickle of freshness – was long over.

I washed off yesterday's sweat in the shower, marvelling at the water that never needed heating. At the end of its journey from the wellhead to my house, it gushed out of the pipe at a perfect temperature: just about blood heat. Exhilaration surged over my skin like the water.

It was thrilling to wrestle with the wounds and exotic diseases of New Guinea tribe folk who sprang to life from the pages of *National Geographic*; but I shuddered as I lathered the soap over my arms and pictured the bloodied and contorted limbs of that little girl in the children's ward.

What had thrown her undernourished body into mortal spasms, shattering the glimmer of response my intravenous fluids had induced? Was it true that those seeds were poisonous?

Scrounging for breakfast among the mostly bare shelves of my refrigerator, I found a papaya.

The over-ripe flesh was fuzzy and mushy.

I still hadn't perfected the knack of rapping on the rind of an unopened papaya to determine whether the fruit was at its peak or past its prime.

After slurping down a mug of instant coffee, I headed out the door and up the avenue, thinking what a sacrilege it was to be drinking Nescafe in this land of cocoa and coffee groves.

Bearing down on me like a ship in full sail, the hospital's ubermeister, Matron Sister Pirmina, descended the avenue with brisk, businesslike steps.

"Finally, Dokta," she called from a distance. "Gut morning."

Only her pale face, forearms, and hands were visible. The rest of her was hidden by layers of white veil and habit.

She wore bifocal spectacles with wire frames, sturdy beige shoes over white stockings, and no smile.

Sister Pirmina strode right up to me. And drew uncomfortably close. Her sweat, glistening on her arms, gave off the smell of milk that is just about to turn sour.

She thrust out her starchy white bosom like a barnyard goose farmers keep to hiss at strangers.

"Well you slept, I imagine," she honked, her hard German accent grating on my nerves. "By seven-thirty, Dokta Werner used to start his rounds. Already now, it is past eight-thirty. Too much late for a young man to be starting his work day."

"But Sister, I was up late last night in the children's ward. With a little girl who…"

"We are having no *buts* at Vunapope, Dokta. Long hours they are expected. That just belongs to it." Her English, though fluent, was often an odd mix of German syntax and two decades-worth of New Guinea Pidgin.

She motioned with the neat stack of linen piled in her arms. "Your house is fresh sheets and towels needing," she said. "To your place I am on my way going."

"Thank you, Sister. I'll walk down and let you in."

"There's no need. I have zuh key. Sister Girhildis and I were there yesterday, certain making that everything was in order."

"Oh," I muttered in surprise. It had never occurred to me that the nuns would come snooping into my house.

"And Dokta, where are zuh crucifixes?"

She'd noticed I'd taken them off the walls. It was the first thing I'd done when I'd arrived, even before unpacking my knapsack and suitcase. Was it bad luck, or some sort of heresy, to touch them?

"I put them away in the sideboard." I could feel my Protestant earlobes flush, then burn.

"Sideboart?" she rasped. "What is zat?"

"The piece of furniture in the front room where you put dishes and things. The crucifixes are on a shelf. Behind the candles." I hoped the candles gave the hiding place an air of respectability.

"Yes... Well, to our motherhouse for proper keeping I take zuh holy crucifixes. And don't lose these towels."

She pointed to the *DR-2* embroidered in the corner of each towel. "They are by our supporters in Germany sent, and belong to zuh house we provide for you."

If I was Doctor-2, then Doctor-1 would be the occupant of the much larger house – currently empty – perched on a knoll at the top of the driveway.

The sun glinted off the varnish on its rosewood steps and wrap-around veranda. Sister Pirmina had called it the *specialist's house* in a reverential whisper when she'd taken me on a tour a few days previously.

Sister turned in the direction of my cottage at the lower end of the driveway and began making her way towards my humble dwelling.

.

Then, she called over her shoulder as she waddled off: "At ten-thirty, Dokta, Sister Assumpta will deliver lemonade to your office. She makes this lemonade with our own Vunapope lemons and you will be needing to drink it. In this very hot New Guinea climate, plenty of fluids you must drink. That just belongs to it."

Shortly before lunch, I pulled off my gloves after draining the breast abscess of a young mother. A nauseating stench filled the operating theatre.

In two weeks, I'd discovered pus lurking inside more parts of the body than I'd ever thought was possible.

I figured the hospital should have been named, not St. Mary's of Vunapope, but Our Lady of Purulence.

My skin dripped with sweat, but my tongue was as dry as burnt toast.

I left the woman, still asleep, in the deft hands of Sister Nina, our German nurse-anaesthetist, and went in search of another glass of Sister Assumpta's lemonade.

"Excuse me, Dokta." A junior nurse had appeared like a phantom at my side. She held a hand cupped over her mouth. "Sister says come right away. To the men's ward."

She paused and avoided my gaze. "Michael Toliman is dying," she whispered. "He cannot breathe."

"Who's Michael..." I started to ask, but the girl was already running across the quadrangle, towards the men's ward.

Michael Toliman. It was curious that the nurse referred to a patient by name, both first and last.

The sick and injured were almost always unknown to us. Villagers and plantation labourers appeared out of the bush, we did our best to patch them up, then they slipped away – one way or another.

Toliman. He would be a Tolai, from the clan that dominated the forests within a 50-kilometre radius of the mission.

This territory was once fiercely guarded by Tolai warriors who, a hundred years ago, feasted on enemy clansmen.

Nowadays, our patients belonged to dozens of clans: people

24

who had made their way here to the Gazelle Peninsula, our eastern tip of New Britain Island, from their ancestral homes in the mountains, valleys, and shores of the mosaic archipelago known as Papua New Guinea.

Two minutes' walk down the hill and across the avenue from the rest of the hospital was the men's ward. It was a cluster of three clapboard cottages set in the mission's expansive gardens of neatly edged lawns, tidy hedges, and weedless beds of vibrant flowers.

Near the entrance to the smallest cottage, Sister Girhildis strutted like a white hen.

The ward's major-domo, Sister Girhildis was a slim version of Sister Pirmina, reaped decades ago from the same vintage of sturdy German novices.

As soon as I was within calling distance, Sister Girhildis shouted "Here, Dokta! Already, Father Schiermann is with him."

I froze. The priest had arrived. He must be administering the Last Rites.

My thoughts raced back to that day fourteen years earlier, when I was eleven years old and the news flashed on our kitchen radio at lunchtime: John F. Kennedy – assassinated – head torn apart by a bullet – given the Last Rites!

The images of mayhem in the back seat of a black convertible, televised from Dallas and printed in the newspaper, had scorched my memory.

I had thought the world was going to end, maybe in a ball of fire, and a Catholic priest would seal our annihilation with the Last Rites.

Michael Toliman must now be dead, or so close to it that it didn't matter.

The priest had arrived on the scene first; it was his show and I had no part in his script.

Besides, I wasn't Catholic and had to stay out of the ward to preserve the sanctity of the ritual.

Toliman's soul might be saved, I reasoned, but there would be no saving his body. I was too late.

Sister Girhildis strode forward and grasped my elbow. "Come," she said, guiding me into the anteroom of the cottage. "Many times, for asthma we have Toliman admitted. But zis is zuh vorst attack I am seeing. The intravenous medicine, today it isn't verking. And our last oxygen tank, it is empty." She steered me to the doorway of the ten-bed ward.

Propped up on the bed to my left was a silver-haired man, eyes closed, lips pursed, face cast in pewter.

His blood, lacking oxygen, suffused his lips with purple. Each breath, a raspy whisper, tormented his bare chest with airless heaves and shudders.

Two women stooped at his bedside, tears dripping off their brown cheeks.

The priest, face stern, stood stiffly by the bed.

His white shirt, unbuttoned at the neck, was no longer crisp; his dark trousers, though pressed with care, were frayed at the cuffs.

Draped over his shoulders was the sacramental symbol of his office, a broad purple ribbon.

He was clutching a string of black beads and a small book, its cover worn and curled.

The tableau that I saw before me was a work of art, a sacred image drawn on canvas or carved in marble. For me to encroach with my stethoscope and pagan fingers would be to clamber over Michelangelo's Pieta clutching a hammer. How could I do it?

As I stared from the doorway, Father Schiermann recited lines that I barely heard and couldn't comprehend.

He drew the sign of the cross in the air and again on the forehead of the unconscious man.

He looked in my direction, and a smile spread across his face like the ripples on a quiet pool struck by a pebble.

"Ah, Dokta. Come in. Join us." His smiling invitation was reassuring and friendly; I'd expected firm and foreboding.

"But..." I replied, still rooted at the doorway and unable to articulate the substance of my disquiet.

"No problem," he said soothingly. "I soon my prayers will finish. We both here have work to do."

He took a step back and beckoned with the hand that had just made the sign of the cross.

In that instant, the wizardly brume that swirled about him evaporated like winter fog. He had broken the spell and had become as sympathetic as a popular high school teacher.

I stepped into the ward, not as an intruder, but as a colleague responding to an urgent summons.

But I still didn't want to get close to his rosary or brush against the purple stole that might be the source of a mystical power.

Pressing my hand on the shoulder of the comatose patient and looking into his face, I launched my own ritual.

"Michael, me Dokta Pennie." I expected no response. He was all but dead.

To my amazement, he opened his eyes and looked into mine. *"Api-nun—Dok-ta."* All he could whisper was good afternoon, releasing a single syllable with each shallow gasp.

Shaking off my surprise, I asked, "Does it hurt anywhere?"

He inched his left arm upward off the bed and aimed a leaden finger toward a spot on his chest, just outside his right nipple. He winced with the movement.

I took hold of his right hand. It felt cold. The pulse was feeble. His fingers bulged at the bases of their nails, a sign of long-standing lung disease.

Amplified by my stethoscope, the left side of his chest wheezed loudly in my ears; but the right side was silent, eerily so.

What had happened? I needed to examine the back of his chest to get a better idea, but he was too weak to move without considerable assistance.

"Sister," I asked, "can you pull Michael forward so I can place my stethoscope between his shoulder blades and have a listen?"

Sister Girhildis grasped his arms and pulled him far enough off the pillows to expose his shoulder blades; she grunted with the effort.

As though tapping on a drum, I rapped on both sides of his upper back with my fingertips and compared the quality of the returning notes.

From the left side came a thud, the sound I'd heard on hundreds of normal chests.

But the right side returned a different tone: clear and hollow, like knuckles striking an empty wooden box.

The right lung, injured by asthma, must have collapsed and shrivelled like a popped balloon.

In place of the lung was a massive air pocket, its tremendous pressure gripping the breathing passages, the heart, and the vena cava in a stranglehold.

"Sister, I think he's got a pneumothorax. On the right side. I've got to needle his chest to let off the pressure. We have to work fast."

"Yah. What are you needing?"

"A Butterfly needle—gauge 21 or 23—the longest you've got. And a litre bottle of I.V. fluid. Take the top off the bottle. But don't pour out the solution."

If my diagnosis were correct, venting the air out of his right chest cavity could save him.

He was barely breathing, his heart barely pumping.

There wasn't enough time to confirm my diagnosis with a chest X-ray. If I had it wrong, he would die: right here, right now.

I listened again. I tapped a final time.

Sister darted out of the room, shooing Toliman's two tearful visitors out ahead of her, like stray cats.

She rushed back carrying a chipped enamel dish into which she'd tossed the needle. It looked like a dragonfly: a sharp point, two wings of green plastic, and a lengthy tail of fine tubing that lay coiled in the dish.

"Where's the I.V. bottle, Sister?"

"It's coming, Dokta," Sister replied in a testy, frustrated tone.

Father Schiermann continued his prayers from the end of the

bed. All I could hear were murmurs from his lips.

It seemed a very long time before a nurse appeared with a plastic bottle, its top crudely severed, contents sloshing to and fro.

"Sister, hold the bottle here, close to his chest," I said. She took the bottle and clenched it with both hands.

I lifted the needle by its wings and dangled the tail end of its tubing over the mouth of the bottle.

Lowering my hand, I let the tubing's free end sink to the bottom like a weighted line.

"Michael," I said, touching a spot above his right nipple. "I'm going to put this needle – *wanpela shoot* – right here. Don't move." I held my breath and thrust into his chest, like a hit-man with a stiletto.

The bottle rapidly filled in a storm of froth.

Sister's eyes widened in amazement: "Dokta! Look!"

The uncorking of any bottle of champagne could never have been greeted with more celebration than I felt at that moment.

The eruption from his chest burst and subsided like spent fireworks, then streams of gentle bubbles percolated from the tubing with the rhythm of Michael's respirations.

The old man blinked and opened his eyes, as though awakening after a heavy sleep.

His unshackled breaths rang loud and smooth. His tongue blossomed from purple-grey to pink, and his pulse pounded with the full force of his unleashed heartbeats.

My heart, still riding a tidal wave of adrenaline, thumped against my throat.

I looked to the foot of the bed for a nod of congratulation from Father Schiermann, but he had slipped out. I felt a pang of disappointment, of pride deflated.

Sister brought me a tray of instruments and an ampoule of local anaesthetic.

I knew our tiny butterfly needle would act only temporarily before it began plugging up and became useless. This meant I had to pierce Toliman's chest wall with a length of sturdy rubber tubing.

The punctured lung would heal over the next few days; until

then, the trouble-causing air pocket would dissipate through the tubing.

With the chest tube inserted, and secured with tape and sutures, I sat on Toliman's bed and studied him once more.

Though his wheezing was loud and heavy, he wasn't gasping. His lips were pink. He was safe.

His skin was almost flawless: no scars, no open sores, no tattoos. His teeth were straight, white, and unstained by tobacco or betel nut.

He looked like a man of letters, a professor who'd been dropped into the jungle on a parachute.

I reached over to the bedside table and picked up his chart, a few dog-eared sheets on a clipboard.

Underneath was a book, a hardback in light blue. *Our Lady of the Sacred Heart High School* was stamped across its front cover. Silver lettering down its spine declared the title and author: *Kidnapped* by Robert Louis Stevenson.

I tossed the medical chart onto the bed and fingered the novel as if shaking the hand of an old friend.

When I was eight, I was confined to bed with a case of measles, complicated by pneumonia and unrelenting fever.

I saw terror strike the faces of my parents when coughing spasms pushed me to the brink of suffocation.

Night after night my dad sat with me, his bow tie undone and dangling from the loosened collar of his dress shirt.

He read from *A Child's Garden of Verses* and recounted the life story of its author, Robert Louis Stevenson.

I was fascinated by the Scottish child who was imprisoned for months in bed by a weak chest, but grew up to write famous books, travel the world in search of a cure for his bad lungs, and build a house in the South Pacific.

Those precious evenings with my dad seated on my sick bed were never repeated; but they inspired me to overcome my natural timidity, to endure the schoolyard hazing over my inability to catch the ball or shoot the puck into the net; and they spawned my fascination with the South Seas.

"Dokta... do you know... of the writer, Robert Louis Stevenson?" Michael asked.

"I sure do," I grinned. "I've loved his books. They made *Kidnapped* into a movie when I was a kid."

"He's buried – in Samoa."

I'd memorized the inscription he penned for his Samoan gravestone. How did it go?

I riffled through the pages of the school edition hardcover, searching for the book's author biographical section.

At last I found it. Right here. It stated: Born Edinburgh, Scotland, 1850. Died Vailima, Samoa, 1894.

For his epitaph:

Under the wide and starry sky,
Dig the grave and let me lie.
Glad did I live and gladly die,
And I laid me down with a will.

This be the verse you grave for me:
Here he lies where he longed to be;
Home is the sailor, home from the sea,
And the hunter home from the hill.

Michael's wheezy words broke the silence between us. "You... from Scotland, Dokta?" A pause. "Dokta – something wrong?"

"Uh? What? Sorry." I cleared my throat with a forced cough. "Well, you could sort of say I'm from Scotland. My father is a Scot. But I was born in Canada. I guess my red freckles give me away."

Michael looked at my bare arms and smiled. "Father Jamieson... from Scotland. He taught me English... reading and writing. Dead, now."

Michael's tubing bubbled peacefully as I patted him on the shoulder.

"I think you should rest, Michael. I'll come back to see you a little later on."

"Thank you… and… God bless you." He wheezed, closing his tear-filled eyes. I squeezed his fingers.

I found Sister Girhildis on the stoop outside the ward, scolding the student nurses. Something about not properly weeding the flowerbeds.

"Sister," I asked, after waiting a moment, "how old is Michael Toliman?"

She laughed. "Oh, Dokta, zuh locals don't know how old they are. About time, they have no idea. Here there are no seasons. No calendars. But Toliman's a *lapun pinis*, an old man already. At least forty-five."

"Forty-five! That's not old, Sister."

"It is *here*."

"How come Toliman reads novels and speaks such good English?"

"His parents were killed during zuh war, after zuh Japanese landed at Rabaul in 1942. Our priests and brothers adopted him, taught him reading and writing. To be a catechist they trained him. To everyone he is known."

"What's a catechist?"

"Dokta!" she clucked. "How are you not knowing what is a catechist? Are you not a good Catholic?"

I said nothing.

"He was for many years a lay teacher. To every village going. Teaching zuh Catechism of zuh Holy Church."

She pulled a white hankie from the pocket of her skirt and wiped the sweat from her face.

"Come," she invited. "Let's have some of Sister Assumpta's lemonade. You are looking like needing it."

3

The Rules of Engagement

Elaine Austen was a beautiful woman, but she was far from radiant when I first saw her.

The comely patient had lost too much blood to impart any blush to her flawless ivory skin and delicate features.

"Oh Doctor, what a relief to see your face," she said as I entered the treatment-room. "But you look so young. Are you really the doctor?"

Though I'd faced that question countless times as an intern, my cheeks burned like lanterns.

"That's right," I nodded, grappling to keep my voice low-pitched and oozing with confidence. "I'm the doc, here." What would she think if she knew the ink on my medical license was only a few weeks old?

She struggled to prop herself up on the rusty examination table, her arms extended behind her. "I was afraid that *again* there'd be no doctor at the mission. I'm feeling pretty crook."

The Australian expression jarred my ears. How had *crook* come to mean sick and miserable?

Her mouth twitched, and her eyes, wide and blue, glistened with tears. "Last time, there were no doctors here," she explained.

"I had to be flown right out of this Pacific purgatory," she continued. "To City Hospital in Cairns. It took five hours, maybe six. I nearly bled to death before we reached the coast of Queensland."

She relaxed her arms, sank onto the table, then smeared the teardrops on her cheeks with the heels of her hands. Her tennis bracelet, studded with too many diamonds for me to count, glinted in the rays of the single fluorescent tube in the grimy ceiling. "I told my husband, *never again*. But here I am..."

I glanced towards the German nun who was standing at the bedside. Sister Agatha had propelled me into this private, but cramped, compartment after summoning me to the maternity ward.

Muscular shoulders strained the seams of Sister Agatha's white uniform, and freckles dotted her massive forearms. Her brown hair was not entirely hidden by her wrinkled veil and wimple, and the heavy down above her lip held beads of sweat. She reminded me of an Arctic Husky: part teammate, part pack leader, part lone wolf.

I cleared my throat and returned my attention to the patient. "Sister Agatha tells me you've been bleeding quite a lot."

"I thought I was past the danger zone," she stammered nervously. "The others happened at ten weeks or so. I'm gone seventeen weeks. I checked the calendar in my kitchen this morning."

"When did…"

She sobbed and blew a torrent into the shreds of tissue clutched in her fist. "Sorry?"

"When did the bleeding start?" I asked.

"At first it was nothing," she sighed. "Just a few tiny spots. But then it got really heavy. Round about lunchtime."

She massaged the side of her belly with the flat of her hand. Her wedding finger flashed a diamond the size of an olive. "Can you give me something for the pain? The cramps are getting worse. And I need another pad. This one feels soaked."

"Where do you come from, Mrs. Austen?"

"New South Wales. Near Sydney."

"But where do you live now?"

"We own Talubar Plantation – over on New Ireland – at the southern tip of the island."

Her head and shoulders shuddered as she was struck by a string of sobs. "It's a lonely place. You can only get there by boat or plane. No roads. Just beach and bush."

Sister Agatha stroked Elaine Austen's brow with a moist facecloth and continued the story for her. "They have no health centre anywhere close, Dokta. To us she was flown just before dark. It is a small seaplane her husband's company has."

Then, a look of disgust came over Sister's face. "Almost, they wouldn't let them take off."

"They said it was too late, that we couldn't make it across the channel before sunset," Elaine rejoined. "But the pilot took off anyway. Without a flight plan. We got here in under an hour, I reckon."

More tears spilled onto her cheeks as she continued telling her story. "My husband had to stay behind with my little girl. If you leave the plantation boys alone, even for one night, they break into the beer, get sparked, and rubbish the place." She closed her eyes. "So… here I am."

Here she was, indeed. I went quickly through my routine: pulse, breathing, tongue, abdomen.

Blood saturated the bulky pad between her legs. "Mrs. Austen," I said in a voice I hoped was reassuring, "I'm going to step outside and have a word with Sister. I won't be long."

"Don't forget something for the pain."

I pulled the door closed behind us and felt my stomach tighten. One of the Irish priests had warned me that Sister Agatha governed every aspect of Maternity with a heavy hand and a fishwife's tongue.

Sister Agatha's two eyeteeth, both capped in polished gold, glinted when she spoke. "A lot of blood, Mrs. Austen has lost."

Now, Sister checked the clipboard she had clutched to her chest. "Her pulse – one-thirty-six it is. And low is the blood pressure – only eighty-eight over fifty-two. Near to shock."

"Yes," I agreed, "the bleeding has to be controlled. She needs a D-and-C." I rubbed the sweat from the back of my neck with my palm. "She's been through this before, poor thing."

"I will start the intravenous," Sister Agatha offered. "Normal saline?" A cry pierced the closed door. "And some pethidine I will bring for the pain. The nurses have prepared for you the trolley of instruments."

I was suddenly hot and cold, dry and sweaty. All at the same time. I struggled to spit the words from my mouth before Sister disappeared through an open doorway. "Sister, I... I've never done a D-and-C." My voice was a stage whisper. "Well, not the entire procedure on my own. I've just assisted."

I followed Sister Agatha into the supply room. It was cramped and musty. "I can't operate on Mrs. Austen," I objected. "She expects a gynecologist."

"If the D-and-C you cannot do, she will bleed to death," Sister Agatha said matter-of-factly.

"But," I protested, "there's a surgeon – and a gynecologist – at that big hospital near Rabaul. What's it called? Munga Regional?"

"It's Nonga." Her face now bore a pinched look, like she had caught a bad smell. "Those government hospitals are so filthy, and so poor the care."

The image of Elaine Austen's movie-star features and lavish jewellery loomed before me. I couldn't do my very first operative procedure on her. Not unsupervised from start to finish. There was no way.

"We can get her to Nonga by road in less than an hour, eh Sister? I'll phone ahead," I said hopefully. "Have them expecting her in our ambulance."

"*Dokta*," Sister said in a chiding tone. She shook her head and pursed her lips into a patronizing smirk. "Already, from the last time I know her. She would refuse Nonga."

She looked at her watch. It had a large face and a massive, stainless steel bracelet. "And by now it's too late. Nonga is not much operating after dark. Their staff are mostly going home to their villages. They are afraid of night spirits."

Sister took a set of keys from her pocket and unlocked the door of a small cupboard above the countertop.

She reached in and plucked out a glass ampoule of pethidine, a powerful narcotic we knew in Canada as Demerol.

"But Sister," I objected, "I, I..."

Her clipboard clattered as she tossed it onto the counter. "Dokta, at Vunapope we have never lost a European mother. All over PNG, we are for our good obstetrics known."

My head filled with the quips my friends had made during the weeks preceding my departure for PNG. "What a thrill for a young fellow like you to be setting bones and performing surgery on your own." "Sounds like an amazing adventure." "Hope you don't end up like one of the young Rockefellers who disappeared there a couple of years ago!" "I heard they still eat human flesh and get that fatal brain disease."

In our arrogance, we'd figured it wouldn't matter that I was no expert in obstetrics, or surgery, or tropical medicine. The patients would be primitive tribe folk who wouldn't know the difference between a certified expert and an enthusiastic guy a year out of medical school. A thousand miles from the nearest city, they'd get my services or they'd get nothing – and surely, I'd be better than nothing.

But now, behind the treatment-room door, dripping in diamonds and hemorrhaging in agony, lay Elaine Austen.

Her private plane had landed in the corner of the universe where the only person who might be capable of saving her was me. She was proof that the rules of engagement were nowhere near what I'd expected. My insides churned as if I'd swallowed a basketball.

Leaving Sister to finish preparing the pethidine, I returned to the treatment-room where the air was thick with the fetor of sweat and the iron tang of fresh blood.

As I looked into Elaine Austen's face, my head spun with anxiety. I grabbed the foot of the table, steadied myself, and told her what she already knew, that the cramps and bleeding called for an urgent D-and-C.

I explained that Sister Agatha was setting things up, that I would start the procedure within a few minutes.

Elaine winced in pain. "You'll put me out, won't you?"

"We'll give you something for the discomfort, but you won't be asleep." She was too close to shock from rampant blood loss for me to be confident she would survive a general anesthetic.

"S'trewth! I wish my husband were here," she exclaimed. "Is anyone ever going to give me something for the pain?"

Minutes later I was masked, gowned, gloved, and staring at the array of steel instruments the nurses had assembled on a dark green sheet. It was a medieval torture chamber set for a cookout.

I fingered the long, slender tongs I would use to reach into the vagina and grab the uterus by its cervix.

The skewer-like dilators lay in an orderly row like a matched set of drill bits of increasing diameter.

The smallest was as fine as a darning needle; the largest would stretch the mouth of a cervix to the width of my index finger. Off to one side was the curette, a menacing thing like a screwdriver with a long shaft. At its tip was a sharp-edged loop for scraping the inside of the womb.

Performing a D-and-C is like scraping the pulp from the inside of a pear through an opening you've made by piercing the stem end of the fruit. You have to do this while the fruit sits at the far end of a dark tunnel too small for your hands to fit inside.

From my D-and-C assisting experience, I knew that if the patient is anesthetized, the procedure is not difficult once you develop a feel for the instruments as they stretch and scrape the tissues.

It's an entirely different matter, however, when the patient is awake, terrified, screaming, writhing, and oozing so much blood that you can barely see where to start.

I slid a wide-billed speculum into the mouth of Elaine Austen's vagina, and mentally reviewed the procedural steps I'd practised in Canada the previous year during a few weeks of assisting the gynecologists.

At the far end of the vagina, as a result of the ongoing miscarriage, the mouth of Elaine's cervix had opened up fairly generously.

It had not, however, opened wide enough to permit passage of the curette into the body of the uterus.

One after the other, I had to force the three largest dilators through the cervix to stretch it wide enough to accept my instruments.

With each excruciating thrust of cold steel, Elaine let out a heart-rattling scream and bounced her bottom against the table.

"Doctor! Sister!" She yelled, "I need something stronger for the pain!" She kicked against the stirrups, her feet thrashing wildly just inches from my head.

I struggled to remain calm. "How's the blood pressure, Sister? Is the I.V. running well?" Supporting Elaine's blood pressure with a brisk stream of intravenous fluid was more important at the moment than abolishing her pain.

Sister Agatha made a dismissive *tsk* with her tongue against her teeth. "Of course. I am having everything under control. Already, the blood pressure it is higher."

Obviously, I wasn't supposed to ask about things at Sister's end of the table.

Once the cervix was open, the most painful part of the procedure was over and I expected to be in more familiar territory.

As part of my internship, I had played the role of assistant at many therapeutic abortions performed on fully anesthetized women, carried out in a similar manner to this D-and-C.

My supervisors usually did the dilation, but they let me help with the curettage – the scraping.

For me, abortions were a necessary evil, and now I was glad I hadn't refused to assist with them.

Elaine's life depended on my skill at delicately but completely scouring her uterus so that it would stop hemorrhaging.

What would the sisters think if they knew I had honed my technique in the abortion suite? That was a secret I could never share at Vunapope.

Blood welled out of the wide-open cervix, filling the far end of the vagina and obscuring my view.

I dabbed furiously with the small, frayed squares of old cotton sheeting – recycled and re-sterilized by Sister's staff – that served as reluctant sponges.

Fresh pools of blood appeared as quickly as I could exchange soaked sponges with clean ones.

"Do you have a suction machine, Sister? I'd like to get a better look down here." I wanted to tell her I couldn't see a damn thing with all this blood in the way, but I was acutely aware that the patient was awake.

"The machine is broken. For a new part we would have to send to Germany. Dr. Werner used to do fine work without it. He said not to waste money on expensive parts."

Dr. Werner must have been some kind of a saint. According to Sister Pirmina, he used to start his tireless workdays at sun-up. Now Sister Agatha was accrediting him with the power of X-ray vision.

How could anyone ever measure up to such a hero, especially one buried under an extravagant headstone in the mission's cemetery?

I grabbed another stack of the sisters' homemade sponges from the trolley and swept them with my forceps across the far end of the vagina. The cervix came into view once again.

Seeing my chance, I grasped the curette, eased it through the cervix's dilated mouth, and began to scrape.

With each stroke inside the womb, broken pieces of fetus and placenta – like raspberries mashed with goldfinch bones – tumbled into the vagina.

The sight of half a tiny ribcage made me gag and wince behind my mask.

I lifted the embryonic remains with a pair of slender forceps and, fragment by fragment, dropped them out of sight into the bucket between my feet.

After a while, the strokes yielded neither placental tissue nor fetal shards. The womb was empty. The bleeding had stopped.

"You can give the shot of ergotamine now, Sister. Let's keep the uterus contracted so it won't bleed anymore." I eased the steel speculum out of the vagina.

"Ouch," Elaine moaned. "Doctor, that thing really hurts. Ouch!"

"Yes," I agreed. "Its sharp edges must have been designed by a man. I'm so sorry about all the pain, Mrs. Austen, but we're all done. You did very well."

I peeled the gloves off my fingers and dropped them onto the trolley of instruments, now a bloodied jumble of metal and cotton. "In fact, you were amazing to cope without an anesthetic."

It was *all* amazing. My first solo operation. A safe and stable patient. A successful performance. Elaine Austen had come expecting first class treatment at Vunapope, and she had found it.

Elaine looked incredulous. "Is it over?"

Sister Agatha unfastened the straps from the stirrups, and I helped her ease the woman's legs down onto the table. "Yes, Elaine," I said. "It's over."

She managed an embarrassed half-smile. "Oh, what a relief to get out of those bloody things."

An overriding sense of relief embraced me, too.

I lightly squeezed her shoulder. "You're out of danger now. You'll feel better after Sister cleans you up a little. That pethidine will help you sleep."

As the tension left my shoulders, they dropped. Confidence flowed upwards from my chest and gave strength to my voice. "You're going to be just fine."

"Thank you, Doctor. Will you call my husband?" She ran her hands backwards through her golden hair. "Tell him no worries. I'm fine. But..." A storm of tears flooded her eyes. "But we lost the baby." She buried her face in the fresh facecloth that Sister had given her, and heaved soundlessly.

An image of the tiny bones I'd plunked into the bucket flashed behind my eyes. The baby was lost indeed.

I took a deep sobering breath, patted Mrs. Austen inadequately on the arm, and left her in Sister's care.

My feet and arms were smeared with blood that had soaked through my gown and splashed up from the floor.

I itched with sweat.

Although I was desperate for a proper shower, it felt good to douse and lather under the stream of cool water at the sink down the hall.

Sister approached me with a light blanket draped over one arm. "I make her comfortable and let her sleep," she advised.

She reached into her pocket and pulled out a scrap of paper. "Here is the telephone number. You call Mr. Austen on his plantation. It is only a radio-phone he has. A lot of noises it makes. You must shout."

I nodded agreement as I read the note.

Sister stroked the blanket on her arm, as if to smooth its creases. "You don't need to tell him she would have lost less blood if more efficiently you'd performed the procedure."

4

In Short Supply

I didn't need an X-ray to know that the man had fractured his tibia and fibula into splinters.

His right leg was bent through the shin like a spruce branch that crunches and folds when you try to snap it across your knee.

I had watched as his two grown sons lifted him out of his red Toyota pickup and carried him to a gurney in our reception area.

His name was stencilled on the truck's side panels: Joachim Tomidal, Vunakokor Village, East New Britain. Painted on the engine hood was a Bird of Paradise, PNG's national symbol, fanning its pink shock of tail feathers.

Each time I approached his leg, Joachim let out several bars of musical howls. *"Oh Dokta, i-pain. Me-got bigpela pain."*

He had dark brown skin that had weathered like old leather, a slim build, and an endearing manner that drew me to him immediately.

His clear eyes communicated self-confidence and a sense of humour. His narrow mouth had only two teeth, which looked like a couple of discarded piano keys. They produced a lisp so forceful that his words sprayed into the air between us. In language that was a watercolour of English and Pidgin, he explained how he had fallen out of a mango tree.

He knew he should have asked one of the village boys – a *liklik manki* – to climb up and pick the fruit, but he had gone after the mangoes himself, missed his footing, and crashed to the ground. Despite his pain and yowls, there was a sheepish twinkle in his eyes that told me he knew how stupid he was to be climbing trees at his age. And now he was putting his trust in me to fix him up.

After ordering a shot of pethidine for Joachim's pain, I bound a temporary splint to the back of his leg and asked the nurses to find a bed in Men's Ward for my new friend. Tomorrow, under anesthetic, I'd set his fracture properly in plaster and use X-rays to confirm the alignment of the bony fragments. It would take several tries to get that leg even close to being straight.

I was writing on the clipboard chart when a crowded minibus buzzed past the window. Sister Pirmina was gesticulating from the back seat of the vehicle where some poor soul was at the receiving end of one of her matronly lectures. It had to be the new American doctor, arriving with his family from the airport in Rabaul. "A good Catholic family, the Morrisons," Sister Pirmina had announced a couple of weeks earlier.

I signed off my note and squeezed Joachim's firm but sweaty palm while we exchanged smiles. "*Leg belong you*," I said, "*bai i-orait.*" I would fix his leg. It would be all right. At least that was what I wanted to tell him, but after six weeks of practising solo at Vunapope, and no time for formal language training, it was still a struggle to get my tongue around the New Guinea Pidgin.

The minibus came to a stop some fifty paces past the hospital, opposite the *specialist's house* – an expansive bungalow fronted by a rosewood stairway that opened onto a wrap-around veranda. Two dazed adults and three children emerged from the shiny white vehicle.

They stood passively on the tarmac in front of what would be their home for the next few weeks. Two orderlies helped the driver unload six suitcases, two cardboard boxes, and a child's stroller. Still, the back of the minibus was half-full of cargo. Had I misunderstood? Perhaps the family was staying four years, not four weeks.

"Mom, it's *so* hot." A teenaged girl flicked sweaty strands of blonde hair from her face. "My bum stuck to that boiling car seat. Ouch! Look – did it rip my skin off?" She pushed aside the hem of her short skirt to inspect the top of her thigh. "Like – haven't they heard of air conditioning in this place?"

A boy of similar age, dressed in blue jeans and a tee-shirt, gave the girl a shove from the back. "Shut up, Cheryl. You've been whining all way from Miami. Who cares about your butt?"

Cheryl stumbled two steps forward. "Mom, Patrick hit me."

A fit-looking man raised a hand, waved his forefinger at his children, and shook his head wearily. "Settle down, you two. Lookit. We're *all* hot and tired, but we're here. Finally." He wore flannel trousers, penny-loafers, and a light blue, Oxford cloth dress-shirt. He had rolled up the bulky sleeves past his elbows. Sweat streamed off his jaw.

His wife swept wavy brown hair from her eyes and studied the sky. Her face crinkled. "Brian! Look at those dark clouds. I'm sure I just heard thunder. Did you see lightning?" She clung to the infant perched on her hip. Crumbs and drool smeared the front of the tot's sweat-drenched sailor suit. "Everyone into the house," she ordered. "There's lightning in that sky."

Sister Pirmina lifted a suitcase by its handle. "Mrs. Morrison, every afternoon the sky is looking like that. At Vunapope we have rarely thunder and lightning. You're very safe here."

"Sister, you're not serious," Judy Morrison objected. "Storm clouds every day? I never trust a sky with dark grey clouds. In Entebbe, it was never stormy. Oh, how we loved our time in Uganda. Cheryl was little, and the climate was perfect. Never stifling like this." She jostled the infant on her hip. "Come on, kids. Real quick. Into the house."

Dr. Morrison noticed my approach. He put down a suitcase and called over his shoulder, "Judy, wait a moment. Kids – we have a visitor."

I shook the pale, extended hand. We traded names. Brian Morrison had a youthful face and thick salt-and-pepper hair, conservatively cut.

"And this is my wife, Judy," he said. "And the kids, Patrick and Cheryl, fifteen and thirteen; Baby Andy, he's thirteen months; and James. Oh my God! Where's James?"

Patrick pointed casually to one of the open doors of the minibus. "Relax, Dad. He's asleep in the back seat."

Was the strain on Judy's face a permanent fixture? "Oh, thank God," she said, relieved. "I thought for sure he'd wondered into the jungle. He's only five. And there must be snakes around here."

I looked away. Vunapope was a paradise of groomed lawns and flowerbeds. Acres of them. The jungle was a long hike away. It would take some effort to get lost in this setting, and there were no dangerous snakes anywhere in New Britain.

Judy turned towards me and fanned her face with her hand. "Hi. Is it always this hot here?" She swatted at a fly buzzing over Baby Andy's head. "Cheryl, get James out of that car real quick before he suffocates. And take him into the house. We can't all stand around here waiting to be struck by lightning."

Three matching cardboard cartons were now sitting on the driveway beside the minibus. It felt like Christmas come early. "That's great, Brian," I said. "You brought a whole lot of supplies, eh? Sister must have told you we're pretty low on sterile gloves and needles."

"That's Andy's baby food in those boxes," Judy called from the lightning-proof safety of the elevated veranda. "Junior pears, strained peaches, and mixed tropical fruit. There's another carton somewhere. Ground pork and peas. His favourite. Can you buy Gerber baby food here? I don't know what we're gonna do if we run out. I won't let Andy eat the other kinds. They're too high in sugar and salt."

I again looked away. Bursting from the gardens surrounding

their house was a salt-free fruit salad: passion fruit, banana, mango, guava, and coconut. It would take less effort to peel a fresh banana than pry open a jar of Gerber's finest processed pears.

"Well anyway, it's great to have you finally here, Brian," I said. "I can't remember the last time I got a full night's sleep. It's the obstetrical emergencies. You know how it is, eh? Everything happens in the middle of the night."

Brian chuckled. "Oh yeah? Afraid I can't help you there. I haven't caught a baby since medical school. Must be fifteen years."

"Oh." I pulled a handkerchief from the back pocket of my shorts and dabbed the sweat from my neck. "What sort of practice do you have back home?"

"GM and Resp at MH and UF. I do mostly COPD."

He noticed my puzzled frown.

"Sorry," he shrugged. "General Internal Medicine and Respirology at Mercy Hospital and the University of Florida. Basically, chronic bronchitis and emphysema."

"You're comfortable with pediatric cases, right?"

"Ha-ha!" he force-laughed. "No way. I went into Internal Med to get away from the kiddies." His shoulders shuddered, and he looked up at Baby Andy, now on the veranda, buckled into his Rolls Royce stroller. "I don't know how anyone can stand watching little ones suffer."

My gut sputtered with a flash of anger at his ridiculous implication.

"How about suturing?" I asked, doing my best to sound cordial, not certain I was succeeding.

His answer held no surprise. "Nope. Can't remember the last time I held any kind of instrument. To be honest, I don't think I can take blood anymore. Technicians do that back at MH."

Sister Pirmina deposited a suitcase at the top of the staircase, descended the steps, and stood close to her American specialist. She tried to launch a smile in his direction, but her teeth were so sharply pointed and her lips so narrow that all that came across was a sneer. "How fortunate we are, Doctor, that you are a specialist professor.

All the way from a world-famous medical school." She looked towards me and her patronizing grin dissolved into a piercing squint. "Dr. Pennie, you will continue to look after Maternity, Children's Ward, Accidents and Emergencies. And perform what minor surgery you are capable of. Dr. Morrison will be the physician-in-chief. I'm sure there is much we will be learning from him."

She looked again at Dr. Morrison, this time with an apologetic frown. "We have missed having a proper surgeon these past few weeks but hope that one will be soon arriving."

"Excuse me, Dokta." A stocky girl in a blue shift and nursing aide's cap had appeared beside me. She puffed breathlessly. "Sorry, Dokta Pennie - Edwina says she needs you. Please come to Children's Ward. *Wanpela pikinini i-got bigpela sick long bel belong em."*

I felt relieved by the interruption and momentarily gratified by her public appeal for my expertise.

But Sister Pirmina never missed a chance to assert her superiority. "Lucy," she honked. "What's wrong with the child's belly?"

The young aide looked down at her feet and sucked on the tip of her forefinger. It was clear she felt too intimidated to say any more.

"It's okay, Lucy. I'll go over there right now." I turned to Brian, who was stooping to lift one of the cartons off the tarmac. "Sorry Brian. I'm going to have to catch up with you tomorrow."

"Sure. No problem. See yah." He stood up and extended the cardboard carton toward his son. "Here, Pat. Take this box into the house. Careful. These Gerber jars are breakable. And real heavy."

A small boy lay before me on the table in the treatment room of the children's ward, eyes wide, cheeks wet with tears. His bloated belly rose above the waist of his torn shorts like a tight balloon. Intravenous fluid trickled through a tube taped to one of his skinny arms. Two student nurses hovered at his side, fear on their faces.

Beside the table stood a woman balancing an infant on her arm as he eagerly suckled her bare breast. With the palm of her free hand the woman smeared the tears of the boy on the table, and shushed him when he whimpered. A toddler, flies buzzing around the mucus that oozed from his eyes and nose, stood naked beside her. He grabbed the soiled hem of his mother's *laplap* and stared at me, his face poised to explode with tears at any second.

A woman of middle years slinked towards me. Her bulky frame over-filled her simple, white nurse's dress. A mountain of fuzzy hair loomed above her broad Tolai face, and like an Abyssinian cat, she observed everything but offered little.

"Hello Edwina," I said. "What's the little guy's problem?" The butterflies in my belly fluttered as I recalled Lillianna, the girl who had convulsed and died under my frantic fingers on this same table a few weeks before.

Edwina threw me a sour look, as if she'd rather be anything but the head nurse of Children's Ward, the only PNG national in a leadership position at Vunapope.

"Diarrhea – with blood in it," she said. "And black vomit." I could barely hear her subdued tones above the hubbub of the busy ward.

I nodded a greeting at the mother and pointed to her son on the table. *"Whattem name belong him?"* I asked. I was so obviously the doctor – the tallish man with white skin and awkward Pidgin – that I didn't introduce myself.

The woman shifted her infant from one breast to the other, directing the nipple with practised fingers towards the baby's mouth. "Oska." There was something familiar about the expression in her eyes and the narrowness of her mouth, but I couldn't place it.

By the rock-hard feel of his tender belly, it was clear that something far more serious than stomach flu or appendicitis was attacking Oska from the inside: massive inflammation. Peritonitis.

"Edwina, ask her if they've eaten pork in the last few days?" Edwina conducted a long, sober conversation with Oska's mother in their Tolai language. There wasn't a word I could understand. The room sweltered. Time felt precious. Oska sobbed. The black vomit in a basin next to his head reeked like a sewer.

Finally, I lifted my hand and caught Edwina's gaze.

She nodded. "Yes."

My ears burned with frustration. "What?" Surely, the woman had said a lot more than yes. "For heaven's sake, Edwina. What'd she say?"

Edwina sighed. "Yes. They ate *mumu* pig a few days ago. At the opening of a primary school."

A *mumu* was an elaborate cookout, a traditional feast for special occasions. I'd seen women wrap hunks of raw pork and sweet potato in wet banana leaves and place them in a pit of fire-hot stones. Men covered the leafy packets with more sizzling rocks and sealed the pit with a mound of earth. After eight hours or so, the men dug up the earth and stones, the women unwrapped the sooty packets, and everyone devoured the feast with bare fingers.

In lowland *mumus*, the women braised the meat, fruits, and vegetables in a sort of ambrosia: a cream they squeezed from coconut meat they grated to a pulp against the sharp edge of a seashell. The exotic blend of flavours, tinged with the cinders of banana leaves, was beyond delicious.

But sometimes, clostridia bacteria within the home-butchered pig meat survived the gentle cooking and produced toxins that attacked long stretches of the bowel. To make matters worse, an enzyme in New Guinea sweet potato amplified the toxin's intestinal destruction. For little children, that spelled a disaster unique to PNG: *pigbel*. If the crucial players—undercooked pork, toxic bacteria, and New Guinea sweet potato—converged in a child's stomach, the nightmare of *pigbel* soon haunted the *mumu* celebrations.

The textbook I kept in my office, and referred to almost daily, described *pigbel* as bloody, excruciating, and lethal.

"Do you think this could be *pigbel*?" I asked Edwina.

I looked at Oska's tormented face and hoped Edwina would return a more appealing diagnostic explanation.

She shrugged and looked away. "Could be." Her obvious reticence – the nuns had tried to assure me that it came entirely from shyness – had the sting of hostility.

I fidgeted with my watchband and scratched where heat and sweat prickled my wrist. "I've never seen it. What's it look like?"

Edwina pulled a small, thin book from the pocket of her uniform. "Look in here."

The blue cover called it *Standard Treatment for Common Illnesses of Children in Papua New Guinea*. I flipped through the pages and found the diseases in alphabetical order. Anaemia. Burns. Croup. Diarrhea. Malaria. *Pigbel*.

For the treatment of *pigbel*, the handbook recommended intravenous fluids to correct dehydration, a stomach tube through the nose to decompress the bowel, and two inexpensive antibiotics— available everywhere in PNG – to treat infection. It advised abdominal surgery only as a last resort to stem uncontrolled bleeding and infection. I didn't like the final words on the page: "Few children survive if they become sick enough to require an operation."

"Okay," I said grimly. "Let's give him the antibiotics. It says here, penicillin and chloramphenicol."

Recognizing the chevrons on her forehead and desperate to be touched by the cool confidence of her bearing, I turned to Veronika, the senior student I'd first encountered the night Lillianna had died. "Veronika, would you organize the stomach tube?"

"Yes, Dokta."

I looked again at the mother suckling her infant, batting the flies that swarmed the toddler beside her, and stroking Oska's forehead. "Edwina, will you explain to Oska's mother what we think is wrong with him?"

"She knows already, Dokta. She's seen *pigbel* before."

Oska's mother moved into Children's Ward and slept on a mat under Oska's bed, her infant at her breast, her other son Jeri cuddled into the small of her back. I tightened with worry before each trip to Oska's bedside. What deterioration might I witness next? Heightened pain? Higher fever? Brisker bleeding? Each sunset inched Oska closer to the ride to Rabaul, where the government surgeon would be forced to open his devastated belly. The attempt at repair would be futile.

On the evening of Oska's fourth day in hospital, an amazing sight greeted me from Oska's bed—Joachim Tomidal sitting upright with Oska and Jeri embraced in each arm. He'd propped his newly cast-clad leg on Oska's pillow.

Joachim beamed a huge grin and rapped on the plaster with his knuckles. "*Ah, Dokta. Leg belong me i-goodpela. Liklik pain tasol.*" His lisp sprayed farther than ever.

I was glad he was pleased with his leg and had only a little pain, but what was he doing on Oska's bed?

He jostled the boys and laughed. "*All-i pikinini belong pikinini-meri belong me. Me-got plenty pikinini.*" These were his daughter's children. His grandchildren. No wonder Oska's mother's face had struck me as familiar. She had Joachim's narrow mouth and wide-spaced eyes.

Oska gave me a shy smile. His fever was down. His abdomen had softened like a ripening papaya; there was no burst of tears when I pressed it. We removed the stomach tube.

The next day, his smile was broad and there was a hint of sparkle in his eyes. His diarrhea had stopped. A couple of days after that, he sipped sweet tea and nibbled a banana.

Edwina's little handbook had proven worthy of its sapphire cover. A gem.

As I watched Oska whispering playfully with his brother, a dark cloud dulled my elation over his recovery. Brian Morrison had scoffed a few days earlier when I had shown him PNG's pocket guide for managing adult patients. "I don't need a little book to tell me how to treat pneumonia. I'm a respirologist, for Chris-sake. Lungs are my specialty. Besides, look – they have the antibiotics all wrong. At Mercy we don't use chloramphenicol anymore. We use gentamicin."

"But that's an expensive drug," I said. "A hundred times the price. And in short supply. We've only got enough gentamicin for one or two patients."

Hadn't our pharmacist, Sister Leora, cautioned him already? Raised in Georgia and now past seventy, Sister had the drawl and gusto of a Scarlet O'Hara. A hunchback contorted her tiny frame. Underneath her bulky habit she was awkward, but surprisingly quick, like a white dove with a broken wing. She would have made it clear that she could get hold of only a few doses of gentamicin at a time, just for unusual cases.

"It doesn't matter," Brian had said. "I told Sister What's-her-name, the old one with the humpback. As long as I'm here, I'm gonna use gentamicin for all serious infections. That's what I used in Uganda. Things can't be any different here."

He didn't want to understand or his ego wouldn't let him. Vunapope was part of an integrated system that depended on all of us to blend together. Our supplies were limited, and we were supposed to set an example for the nursing students. After graduation, they would be posted to remote health centres where they would have to look after serious cases with the handbook lighting their way. They would be lucky to have even the most basic supplies in their cupboards. They'd have no doctor to turn to, and no gentamicin.

How quickly would Brian Morrison consume all of our gentamicin? A few days? A couple of weeks? It was inevitable. And a new shipment would take months to arrive from overseas.

The following Saturday, while I was preparing my breakfast, a bunch of overripe bananas caught my eye. I'd bought them a few days earlier from an old woman sitting at her tiny roadside stall. Each fruit, now heavily blemished with black scars, was too gooey and slimy for eating. I could almost feel my mother's words, engraved on my conscience: "I hate seeing perfectly good food go to waste."

The bananas were no longer perfectly good, but I couldn't throw out a dozen of them. Not when the children's ward was full of skinny kids who were seldom given enough to eat. I riffled through the paperback cookbook I'd brought from Canada and found a recipe from my university days. Banana cake. The page was splattered with grease and dried sugar.

I would mash the bananas, make two cakes, and take one up to the Morrisons as sort of a goodwill offering.

Although we hadn't yet had a quarrel, I regretted the lack of any bond between us.

The cake turned out perfectly, neither lopsided nor burnt. It was the first dessert I'd seen in two months; the batter had tasted delicious. I proudly ascended the steps to the Morrisons' veranda with the cake in my hands.

Judy heard my knock and opened the door. "Oh, hi…uh, Ross. How-yah doin'?" Baby Andy was perched on her hip. "Brian's not here. He's over at the hospital." She rolled her eyes. "As usual. This was supposed to be a kinda vacation, but he's at that hospital till five o'clock every day."

"Actually, I just came to say hello and bring you this cake."

"Did you hear the news on the radio? Elvis is dead."

"Elvis?"

"Elvis Presley. The King." She pulled a tissue out of her skirt pocket and dabbed at her face. "I don't know what happened. They didn't give any details. Just said he passed away yesterday in Memphis."

Maybe I'd been born too late to appreciate Elvis, but Judy's tears struck me as foolish and misplaced. I sensed no connection between Memphis and Vunapope, as though the two places didn't even share the same planet.

"I'm sorry, Judy," I said, feeling a bit guilty for my lack of empathy, but more disconnected than ever from the Morrisons of Florida. "Were you a big fan?"

"Uh-huh. I bought all his albums. Brian will be shocked. We used to dance to *Love Me Tender*."

She looked at the plate in my hands. "They sure have funny-looking cakes here, huh? I guess they don't know about frosting. How come it's square, not round?"

"All I could find in my kitchen was a square pan. I think it'll taste all right, though. It's banana. Fresh out of the oven."

"You mean, you made it? But where'd you get the cake mix from?"

"It's not from a mix, I made it myself."

"No mix? Ross, you're kidding me. I've never made a scratch cake. I wouldn't know where to start."

She could start at the first line of the recipe and go from there. "It wasn't difficult," I said with a shrug. "It only took a few minutes."

"I wouldn't be able to get this oven to work. It's gas. Our stove in Miami is electric.

"No problem. The oven's easy to light. You strike a match and put it in the little hole at the bottom. Here – I can show you..."

"No thanks, the house might blow up." She said, backing up towards the door. "I'm gonna stick with the electric frying pan and the toaster." Her shoulders sagged. "I wish we'd brought my electric range. We really should've. It's a beauty. Avocado-green. With an oven big enough to fit a twenty-five-pound turkey."

"Should I put the cake on your kitchen table for you guys to try later? You look like you've got your hands full."

Judy stood on guard at the door. "No. It's okay. Cheryl will take it. Patrick's in his room with the drapes pulled. He's got a terrible sunburn. Huge blisters across his shoulders. I can't believe how strong the sun is here. He never woulda got a burn like that in Florida."

She called out to her daughter through the window screen. The girl pushed open the door, took a quick look at the cake, and sneered as she and her mother retreated into the house. I took the cake back to my house.

Oska stayed in the children's ward for three weeks. It took that long to restore his strength. Joachim, his grandpa, made frequent visits to the ward and delighted in the boy's progress. He was proud of his own facility with the crutches that Sister Girhildis had produced from a dusty storeroom in the men's ward. He brought me a cornucopia of mangoes, watermelons, pineapples, and an occasional fish, each time tapping his cast and flicking his eyebrows in approval of my handiwork.

As Oska's condition improved, his mother's shyness faded into chaste flirtatiousness. When she saw me coming, she would throw on her smock-like top, covering her breasts with a billowy PNG *meri-blouse* that flashed a melee of printed birds and flowers.

When the time approached to send Oska home, I came to check his chart and examine his tummy. Instead of Oska in the bed, it was Jeri, his younger brother with the nose that dripped like an open faucet. He lay wide-eyed but motionless on the mattress. He burned with fever. Sticky green pus oozed from his left ear. His earlobe was swollen, and it jutted from his head at an odd angle. Behind it, the skin was red and boggy; when I touched him there, he screamed. He had all the signs of acute mastoiditis, an infection of the skull bone behind the inner ear. Jeri was one step away from an abscess invading his brain.

Veronika, the senior student, heard Jeri's wail. "Good afternoon, Dokta. Oska is playing outside. But Jeri is sick. I swabbed his ear two days ago when I saw the pus. The fever started this morning."

She handed me a square of paper, crinkled and folded. "Miss Janet brought this over today."

Janet Lundquist was our hospital's laboratory technologist. She had grown up in an iron-mining town in northern Minnesota, and her two-year PNG posting, coincident with mine, was her first job out of university. Although she had ventured to Vunapope via the bureaucracy of the Catholic Medical Missions Board, she had confided that she couldn't remember the last time she'd been inside a church. She shared my interests in hiking, snorkelling, and photography. From her first moment on the job, Janet had thrust her natural enthusiasm into the laboratory. She coped with the capricious cuts in electricity and the shortage of supplies; she reorganized the mess left by her predecessor, an elderly nun who had been persuaded to retire.

Since Brian Morrison had arrived, Janet's workload had quadrupled.

"You know, Ross," she had said, "that guy orders more blood tests in a day than I can possibly perform in a week."

She'd complained to Sister Pirmina – whom she'd nicknamed Sister Piranha – that Doctor Morrison was demanding more than the laboratory could handle.

56

I chuckled to myself as I remembered Janet mimicking Sister's caustic reply. She mimed Sister's mannerisms: a hand on one hip and a forefinger wagging towards heaven. "You must ask Our Lord for zuh strength you are needing. Doctor Morrison is coming very highly qualified. He's a university specialist. A good Catholic husband. Vee must give him vhatever he vants."

We had quoted Sister's closing mantra in unison: "That just belongs to it."

On the wrinkled slip of paper, Janet's handwriting was neat, and her message was clear. "Jeri Tomanga, Children's Ward, swab of left ear, *Pseudomonas aeruginosa.*"

Oh no. Not *Pseudomonas*. It was a nasty germ susceptible to a limited number of expensive antibiotics. Jeri would need gentamicin. Nothing else in our pharmacy would work. Without it he would die a terrible death: pain and pus and paralysis.

But Brian Morrison had used up all the gentamicin. Every single vial. He'd told me so himself, not long after I'd brought over that cake. He'd been angry about being coerced into following the handbook's instructions and using old-fashioned medicines.

Fury roiled from my stomach into my throat. Sister Pirmina's hotshot American specialist had exhausted our gentamicin. Now Jeri was going to pay the price. I wanted Brian Morrison gone. I'd look after every patient in the hospital, day and night, if only he'd take his whiny family right back to the States where they belonged. Back to their avocado-green electric range, their Elvis Presley albums, their air-conditioned life in Miami.

My watch said two-thirty. Damn. The sisters would all be in their convent, napping away the day's oppressive heat. Anyway, there was no point in voicing my distress to Sister Pirmina. She would delight in reminding me that Doctor Morrison was a highly qualified *specialist* – that every day he attended Mass, his every duty guided by *Our Lord*.

Janet would be sleeping, too. There was no one who could help me ventilate my steam. I stomped home.

At four o'clock I found Sister Leora at her dispensary counter.

By then the indignation had drained out of me.

I no longer cared if Brian Morrison stayed or went, I was simply in despair over Jeri.

I explained my predicament, my voice getting higher with each sentence. "I hate seeing him suffer like this," I concluded. "Is there any way you can scrounge even a few doses of gentamicin?"

"Well now, young fella. Calm down. It's okay. I saw that Yankee specialist a-comin' a mile off. Boston accent and all. The Civil War taught us Southerners a thing or two about survival, you know. I put a few boxes of gentamicin outta sight for a rainy day." She tapped her nose with a gnarled forefinger, looked through the window at the cloudless sky, and let out a giggle. "I hid them behind all the packets of birth control pills the government sends us but we never use. Sister Pirmina and Doc Morrison would never think of looking there."

I followed her, grinning widely. Sister Leora was a godsend.

She pointed a flashlight towards the nether regions of her storeroom. "Come on. I'll show you where I hid 'em. There's plenty enough to treat a youngster, even for a few weeks."

She wobbled between the rows of shelves like the injured dove that she was. "Pseudomonas, you say? We're also gonna raid my stash of carbenicillin. You're gonna need that, too, I reckon. Jeri's gonna be okay. You'll see."

5

The Expats

On Saturday mornings, unless there were emergency cases that couldn't be put off for a couple of hours, I routinely drove into Rabaul to shop for my groceries.

There were three supermarkets: Steamship's, Burns Philp, and Anderson's.

Each would be out of stock of different items at different times and in a perennial state of anticipation of the next cargo ship.

By stopping at all three, I could usually find everything I wanted, including vanilla ice cream, Campbell's soup, and Miracle Whip salad dressing, my personal staple.

The first time I spotted the jars of Miracle Whip for sale at Anderson's, I bought four of them, thinking that such a miraculous appearance was unlikely to be repeated.

Rabaul's open-air market swelled on Saturdays into a choppy sea of brown faces, toothless smiles, and brightly printed meri-blouses.

Scores of women squatted on mats beside pyramids of homegrown fruits and veggies. At least one woman would mumble "Morning, Dokta," place a hand over an embarrassed smile, and lift a pineapple, papaya, or handful of tomatoes towards me. If I offered money, she'd shake her head and pull in her hands.

The *Café de Paris* beckoned like an oasis from its blue and white façade on Casuarina Avenue. It offered gingham, lace, and air conditioning in an otherwise brash and sweltering frontier town. Two effete Australian guys ran the place but kept to themselves. I wondered what had provoked their escape to New Britain – generations of hometown homophobia or a particular humiliation?

I was sure to encounter a familiar face or two in the café, from our community of expatriates. We expats came in three versions: European, Chinese, and Filipino. All whites in PNG were called *Europeans;* a term I felt bestowed on us an undeserved tone of gentility.

I thrived on being part of New Britain's cosmos, of running into familiar characters on almost every corner; and I glowed in the special status I achieved by being privy to the intimate details of their digestive problems, the unrelenting itch of their athlete's foot, or the heartbreak of their unspoken infertility.

It was said that all expats in PNG were Mercenaries, Missionaries, or Misfits. While I stirred my cappuccino, I wondered which of those M-words described me best.

A car could travel for only an hour at most in any direction from Vunapope. Beyond that, pavement dissolved into riverbeds; graded gravel scuttled onto muddy jungle footpaths. Close to home, the golf course at Kokopo and the coral-studded beaches provided most of my diversions.

For fifty dollars a year I joined the Kokopo Golf Club. The nine-hole course undulated under the coconut palms on a strip of scrubland bordering the sea.

On Thursdays the expat wives put together a home-cooked supper, usually a variation of curried mutton or mysterious cuts of barbecued meat.

They assured me that the steaks and chops sizzling on the grill were fine Australian beef and lamb, but the cuts always had the chew of oxen that had succumbed after decades of overwork.

One Thursday evening, a few weeks after the Morrisons had packed all their things and returned to Florida, I toyed with a plate of stew and watched the bustle of diners, cribbage players, and heavy drinkers at the tables around me. I could feel the early stages of a migraine boring into my head, like a phalanx of woodworms. Feeling the need to be alone in anticipation of rising nausea and a pounding forehead, I settled into a chair at the edge of the rectangular concrete slab that served as the clubhouse floor.

Our club had no walls, just a corrugated tin roof to protect us from the sun, the rain, and the coconuts that crashed to the ground like cannon balls. At one end, the industrial refrigerator hummed behind the wet bar, both to be secured behind steel shutters when the last of us went home.

The darkness of night pressed in and gave the place the impression of four walls that didn't exist during the day. The rectangular dimensions, and the fluorescent light tubes that hung on cords from the rafters, created the illusion of an aquarium.

It struck me that the expats of the Kokopo Golf Club swam around the tables like the creatures of the coral reefs that ringed the islands of PNG.

The elderly Mr. and Mrs. Arthur Hadley-Rix held court in the centre of the action, perched like monarchs on twin thrones. White-haired, and dressed in layers of white linens that evoked a bygone era of tropical formal dress, they resembled a pair of sedentary sea anemones.

Their two daughters-in-law fussed around them like sycophantic clownfish, refreshing their drinks, offering them second helpings of salad, and lighting their cigarettes.

The last time I'd seen Mr. Hadley-Rix, he'd been at home in bed, delirious with fever. Sister Pirmina had insisted I make a house call. My first one.

"He's an old man," Sister had said. "From Australia, but for many years living in Kokopo. I am seldom demanding that he come to the hospital when a sickness strikes him."

All but hidden behind exuberant vines of purple bougainvillea, their expansive bungalow overlooked the ninth tee of the Kokopo golf course. Gardens overflowed with orchids that shouted every possible pattern and hue, a visual orchestra over which Mrs. Hadley-Rix waved a celebrated jazz baton.

I found the old man in his four-poster bed, its mosquito net folded back neatly. His face dripped with sweat.

His eyes filled with terror. "Fifty zorros approaching from the south-east," he shouted. "Did you read me? Fifty bloody zorros."

Mrs. Hadley-Rix read the puzzlement on my face and touched my arm. "He's still haunted by Ferdinand. It comes out every time he has a fever."

I scrunched my eyebrows, wondering who Ferdinand was, and gave Mr. Hadley-Rix an injection of antibiotic for his pneumonia.

I helped his wife tuck him inside the mosquito net and followed her to the living room. She directed me to a comfortable seat and told me the story of their life in PNG.

Long before World War II, the newly wedded Betty and Arthur Hadley-Rix boarded an Australian cargo ship bound for New Britain. They debarked at Vunapope Wharf, waved goodbye to the captain, and set to carving a coconut plantation out of the jungle near Kokopo.

"In those days, Kokopo was just a five-shack hamlet down a muddy track from the mission," she explained.

Just before the attack on Pearl Harbor, when the Japanese invasion of New Guinea became a dread-filled certainty, Betty and their two small boys sailed to the safety of Queensland.

Arthur remained in New Britain throughout the war.

As a coast watcher, an Allied civilian, he hid in the bush behind enemy lines and radioed clandestine reports of Japanese ship and aircraft movements: Project Ferdinand.

"My Arthur suffered months of malnutrition and dysentery," Betty sighed.

"He lived in primitive bivouacs and didn't have dry feet for three years. Appalling. If they'd ever captured him, the Japs would have tortured him horribly. Then executed him. On the spot."

"What was he shouting about zorros?"

She looked puzzled. "Zorros? Oh, you mean the Zero. The Japanese single-engine fighter plane. The skies were full of the bloody things. They pranged them into the bush all over New Britain. There's one at the Coast Watcher Memorial on the overlook above Rabaul. It's mostly intact. Worth a look."

While I sat in a calico armchair in her air-conditioned living room enjoying lemon cookies from a porcelain plate, Betty described how they had rebuilt their plantation after the war. The place had been destroyed by the American bombardment of Japanese encampments. Her sons later expanded the plantations and took up cocoa production.

"Chocolate pays much better than coconut," Betty said. "But in 1975, PNG became a *sovereign nation.*" She rolled her eyes at what she clearly viewed as a brazen designation. "And they forced us to give up our Australian passports. Become PNG citizens or forfeit our holdings of a lifetime."

"They wouldn't let you have dual citizenship?"

She raised an eyebrow and shook her head. "No, my dear. All or nothing. We were like Portia's suitor. You know, in *The Merchant of Venice?* We chose to give and hazard all we had." She sighed and dropped her shoulders. "Then we paid the bishop in advance for our two plots in Vunapope's cemetery."

Enveloped by the printed vines and cabbage roses of the overstuffed sofa, her bony frame had looked painfully fragile…

Now my attention was diverted back to the present and to Dawna Wallis as she darted from table to table in the clubhouse reef. She spooned rice salad from a large wooden bowl onto one plate after another, chatting and laughing with everyone she encountered.

She was a parrotfish in a sundress of bright red, blue, and yellow. She and her husband Garnet had grown up together in Swift Current, a prairie town in Saskatchewan. They'd come to teach at Kokopo High School immediately after their university graduation. They loved the Kokopo life so much that they'd signed on for a second two-year term with CUSO, the Canadian aid agency that was also sponsoring my posting.

A week earlier, Dawna had visited my outpatient clinic because of a sore throat and a nasty cough. Although healthy breath sounds echoed from her chest into my stethoscope, I paused and cleared my throat as I lifted the instrument from my ears.

Ever since first meeting Dawna, I'd wanted to ask about the scars on her left foot and to hear how she'd lost her fifth toe. The skin below her ankle puckered like egg white splattered across a hot pan. She walked with a limp, which only a mother or a doctor would notice. Now that she was my patient, I hoped it wasn't voyeurism to ask for the history behind the obvious surgery, skin grafts, and amputation.

"Oh, there's quite a story there, Ross," she said. "I was eleven years old, visiting the Calgary Zoo with my parents and all five of my brothers and sisters. I was wearing my brand new plastic flip-flop sandals – thongs, as we used to call them – and I was so proud of them. Mine were pink and white. And, for once, not hand-me-downs. Anyways, the gorillas fascinated me and I went right up to their cage. A huge male grabbed me by the foot, pulled my entire leg through the bars, and chomped down hard. My brother said the ape held my foot with both hands and chewed it like a sandwich. I guess I screamed a lot and passed out. I remember a huge white bandage on my leg when I woke up in the hospital. I was heartbroken that my beautiful pink sandal had disappeared."

I stared at her foot, imagining the anatomy of the destruction and the task the surgeon had faced. "My God, Dawna. What an experience."

She nodded grimly. "For weeks I cried every night, knowing that they shot the gorilla because it wouldn't let go of me. I felt so guilty. Of course, my brother wasn't supposed to tell me they killed the gorilla. Or that my flip-flop had gotten chewed to bits."

Dawna's face had been calm, peaceful, even maternal. "I hardly ever think about it now. When people at home asked why I wasn't afraid to go live in New Guinea where there used to be cannibals, I just said that if you can get your foot nearly bitten off by a gorilla in the Calgary Zoo, there's no point in staying home. You might as well see for yourself what the world's got to offer."

If Dawna was the extroverted parrotfish, then Garnet was the less colourful mackerel swimming about the Kokopo reef. Dependable and energetic, he devoted himself to the smooth running of the golf club. He would never set the world on fire, but at the first sign of flames he would be on the frontline gripping the fire hose in his hands, the satisfied smile of the volunteer on his face.

Seeing me sitting in the corner by myself, Garnet left his beer on the bar and walked over to my table.

"Dawna's cough cleared up really fast on those antibiotics you gave her, Doc," he said. "Thanks a lot. What're you drinking? A *San Miguel* or a *South Pacific*? My shout."

"No beer for me just now, thanks Garnet." Alcohol would speed up the migraine's hammers pulverizing my brain. "But... But a gingerbread – sorry a ginger *ale*, would be nice."

He looked at me quizzically, as people did when a migraine caused my face to blanch like chalk and my words to stumble out of my mouth like drunken sailors.

"You're sure? One beer won't dull your professional senses, eh, Doc?"

Ginger ale did seem thin and juvenile compared to the parade of beers and vodka cocktails that were crossing the bar and into the hands of the Thursday evening crowd. Even when I didn't have a headache, I couldn't imagine drinking so much and still standing.

"A ginger ale will be fine, Garnet. Got a terrible headache."

"Do you need any painkillers? I can ask Dawna. She's gotta have some in her purse, eh?"

"It's okay, Garnet. Already took some. And tell Dawna thanks a lot for the batch of brownies she brought to my office the other day."

From behind Garnet's shoulder I caught sight of an Australian white-tip shark circling the tables. In his fist he held a beer, which he thumped down to punctuate his outbursts and expletives. Roger Hunter had sun-weathered skin, a well-fed belly, and dark khaki shorts that were so brief that they threatened to show off his buttocks. His shirt, unbuttoned halfway to his navel, exposed more of his hairy chest than I cared to see. He ran a hand back through his thick black hair and unfurled his broad white forelock, which fluttered above his rogue brow like a skull and crossbones.

He raised his bottle to me in a mess hall salute. "Good day, Doc. Why so glum? You look as happy as a bastard on father's day. Afraid I'm gonna make you blush again?"

My cheeks never flushed in the middle of a migraine. Today, I could look him straight in the eye.

He wiped a glob of spittle from his lower lip with the back of his hand. "What's your poison, Doc?"

"It's okay, Roger. Garnet's getting me a drink. Thanks anyway."

"But I owe you one. Fair dinkum." He hitched the zipper of his fly with a quick tug. "Back in working order, thanks to you." He stroked the side of his nose with his forefinger and eyed his latest conquest, a Tolai girl he'd left to sit by herself – a jellyfish stranded on dry sand, motionless and fearful.

"Be sure to let me know when you're ready for your next beer."

Roger chugged from his bottle and headed toward another table of drinkers. I forced myself to keep looking at his bloated face and not let my eyes stray towards the crotch of his shorts. Last week I'd seen what lay inside it.

He had driven to the hospital complaining to the nurses that he had abdominal pain. But Roger had refused to be seen by anyone but "the Doc." As soon as we were alone in the examining room, he planted his feet and pulled down his fly. "My jimmy's covered in sores, Doc," he said as he popped his flaccid penis out of his shorts.

It was the biggest one I'd ever seen. By far. I didn't know that anyone could have an organ *that* size. My cheeks and ears began to redden at the sight of it.

Roger chuckled – he could tell what I was thinking. My damnable blushing, arriving unbidden and with such blatant visibility, had unmasked my private thoughts, throwing me into a too familiar cycle of accelerated embarrassment. I felt like a lantern.

"Hey Doc, by the colour of your face, I'd wager you've never seen a man's member that big."

I didn't answer. I couldn't. I turned my back and grabbed a pair of gloves from a drawer. After a few deep breaths I turned around, kept my head down, and set about a professional examination of his penis.

Thick yellow pus oozed from its tip, and red patches of denuded skin marred its shaft, as if a barracuda had thrashed his manhood. It was gonorrhea and chancroid, two sexually transmitted diseases in a chorus line of similar infections he shrugged off as the single man's battle scars.

I shot two syringes of penicillin into his buttocks and scribbled a prescription for a week's worth of antibiotic tablets. As the owner of Rabaul's only pharmacy, he could count the pills out for himself.

"You know, Roger, you should always use a condom. You've got them in your own pharmacy, for heaven's sake."

"Ah, Doc. It just wouldn't be the same with a rubber."

My face still felt hot, but it didn't matter any more. "Jeez, man. What kind of germ are you going to pick up next time? One of these days you'll get something nobody can treat."

"No worries, Doc," he had said, tucking in his shirt. "She'll be right..."

A burst of laughter in the clubhouse drew my attention to the most flamboyant pair in the place, Jack and Emaline Randall, our much-anticipated surgeon and his wife. They had not so much arrived at Vunapope as danced in like retired vaudevillians. Loud and proud, they had settled in immediately.

Emaline may have spent her forty years of marriage in a town in the shadow of the Canadian Rockies, but her accent, fluid movements, and layers of bangles and lace proclaimed that her soul had hatched in New Orleans.

She was the psychedelic coral trout of the Kokopo reef –

flamingo stripes, fuchsia swirls, and a canary boa that floated on the breezes. Stories, embroidered with endless detail, flowed from her generous mouth with its glossy red lips.

Her husband, Jack Randall – "Call me Jack! Dr. Randall was my granddad." – had dressed himself in what you could loosely call an outfit: a matching shirt and shorts of brown and orange paisley polyester.

Jack occupied the reef's *Charonia tritonis*, the triton shell that village men plucked from the sea and blew like a trumpet to signal their clansmen across the valleys. While under the water, the triton was the king of the reef, the prized but quiet giant. It acquired its compelling voice, however, only after it lost its inner substance and became a hollow shell.

Working alongside Jack Randall in the operating theatre, I'd heard plenty of his bluster. At the start of a hysterectomy or a Caesarean section he'd look at me over his bifocals and say: "My granddad always said you had to handle a scalpel like a woman. Be firm with her and act confident. And if you don't take her for granted, she'll let you go all the way."

While Jack basked in Sister Pirmina's adulation of *The Surgeon,* I was just the assistant. The unacknowledged lackey who intervened when failing eyesight brought Jack close to cutting vital structures or to leaving bloodied sponges inside patients' bellies.

Without warning, the Kokopo clubhouse went black and silent. The refrigerator stopped humming. All conversation ceased. The ceiling fans stopped whirring. My nose came alive with the scent of frangipani blossoms. The silky touch of the tropical air, now calm, settled like a soothing hand on the nape of my neck. The hammers in my head were put to rest. A moment of bliss.

Someone shouted the obvious: "There's been a power cut."

Someone else giggled.

The narrow beam of a pocket flashlight tore through the peaceful dark.

"I'll get out the hurricane lamps, eh?" said Garnet Wallis.

"They're in the storeroom."

"I'll give you a hand, mate." There was a creak as an athletic but invisible frame pushed itself out of a chair; metal scraped against concrete. "No worries." No mistaking Kent Eastman's accent, Australian at its richest.

Kent's mechanical wizardry kept the Catholic mission's multimillion-dollar logging business operational.

In a land where heavy equipment broke down every day and spare parts were impossible to locate, he could repair bulldozers and tractors with wire, washers, and widgets.

Like the coral reef's hermit crab that moved into damaged and abandoned seashells, Kent Eastman could live anywhere and fix anything.

He read Shakespeare for fun and had consumed every word that Wilbur Smith had ever published.

The flashlight's beam flitted across the dark clubhouse and disappeared at the far end. Cupboard latches clicked, doors banged, Kent and Garnet muttered. The beam swept the clubhouse once again, and the two men plunked whatever they'd retrieved onto a table.

"I've got some matches," a woman's voice said. A soft glow flared before her face as she tiptoed over to the table, a flame cupped in her hand.

More matches flared and died. A succession of disappointments. In the light of each brief flame, glints reflected from the glass chimneys of four old-fashioned lamps.

The lamps wouldn't light; their wicks would not hold a flame.

"There's no fuel in any of these lamps," Kent said. "The lamp spirit – the meths – has evaporated."

"Sorry everyone." Garnet's tone was defensive. "But you know, eh? It's been a while since we last had a power failure, eh? A couple of weeks, anyways."

"No worries. I reckon there must be some meths in a bottle back in that cupboard," Kent said. "Hand me your torch again, Garnet." With that, Kent made his way to cupboard.

Moments later, distant sounds of boxes and bottles being shifted about echoed in the warm night air.

Kent's confident footsteps soon signalled his return. "I think this is the meths." Something heavy struck the tabletop. "It's hard to tell in the dark, but it doesn't smell like the petrol for the mowing machines."

"Let's have a look," Roger Hunter grunted. "Gimme the bloody torch."

A large plastic jug glowed in the wavering beam of the flashlight, now gripped in the pharmacist's unsteady hand.

"Yeah. It's meths, all right," Roger said. "You can see it's the same blue-coloured stuff I sell in my shop. Methylated Spirits. The kanakas drink it in their villages when they run out of beer." A burp rumbled in his throat. "I tell them it's poisonous, that it's just for their lamps. But they're such stupid buggers..."

The refuelled hurricane lamps smoked and glowed with a dim and mellow charm.

In celebration, our own crew of stupid buggers snapped the caps on another round of beers and guzzled them down.

The cribbage players drew close and continued their game within a circle of flickering shadows, and before a beer could be pressed into my hand, I slipped out towards the comfort of my bed.

6

The Formula

The operation was taking longer than Jack Randall had said it would. My back was stiff. My calves ached.

It was long past lunchtime and my stomach groaned in rebellion. Jack, who had worked with me throughout the surgery, also looked worse for wear.

In a basin on the counter lay the object of our quest, an ovarian tumour that glistened like a deflated beach ball smeared in motor oil. It was a cyst so large we'd had to drain off eight litres of its fluid before there was room for us to manipulate it safely from the anesthetized woman's abdomen.

We'd stood and waited with bloodied hands, while Sister Nina had rummaged in a cupboard, retrieved a length of rubber tubing, and sterilized it in a pan of boiling water. Finally, we'd thrust the tube into the cyst, watched the viscid contents swirl into a bucket on the floor, and hauled the tumour out.

"She's going to be very pleased when she wakes up," I said, inserting the first of a double layer of stitches that would close our incision. The wound ran the full length of the woman's belly, and I had to make sure each knot was tight and square. Jack would growl if a knot wasn't perfect. "She'll have a nice flat tummy," I concluded. "And she'll be able to see her toes."

"I'll say," Jack agreed with a laugh. "The old girl was afraid she might be pregnant," he noted, pulling off his gloves. "Wondered why no baby had come out after two years."

Sister Nina shook her head and adjusted the dials on her anesthetic machine. "Dr. Jack… already her youngest is in high school. She knew her childbearing was forever finished."

Jack chuckled again and turned around to allow Sister Nina to untie the back of his gown. He slipped into the pantry where we left our street clothes and emerged a moment later hitching the belt in his white Bermuda shorts. "Everything okay with those stitches of yours, young fellah?"

I rolled my shoulders and stretched my neck, coaxing kinks out of my back. "A few deep ones left to go. Then just the skin."

Jack pulled up baby-blue knee-socks and strode to the door. "I'd better scoot. You'll take care of the post-op orders, eh Ross? Emaline won't be happy if my lunch is ruined." With that he left.

I shrugged in response. I'd worked through so many meals that I'd had to punch a new hole in my belt to hold up my shorts. It was ages since I'd last been grocery shopping. My stomach rumbled again at the thought of the naked shelves in my fridge and kitchen cupboards. The aroma of buttered toast, the sharp taste of marmalade, the crackle of fried eggs and bacon swirled in my head.

"Dokta!" chided Sister Nina. "Might we finish today?"

"Sorry, Sister. Almost done."

I set to looping and knotting the final sutures. When I'd finished, Sister handed me the bandage she'd prepared and I pressed it into place. Finally, I could pull off my gloves and shed my sweaty gown.

The patient coughed and groaned in a noisy awakening. I wrote her post-op orders, changed my clothes, jumped into my Toyota, and roared off in search of the fixings for my lunch. There was no fast food in Kokopo; no slow food, for that matter. But until late in the evenings there was Henry Chen behind the counter of his trade store. Seven days a week.

The unpaved parking lot in front of *Chen's Kokopo Variety* was a junkyard of discarded pull-tabs and bottle caps. Coca Cola,

Fanta, and SP Lager logos glinted on the trampled earth. My flip-flops crunched on candy wrappers and slid over cigarette butts.

I pulled open the door of the cave-dark shop. A sharp voice bellowed from the nether regions. "You got your lollies, now get out." Henry had no patience with kids who rummaged through his shelves, more in search of fun and mischief than biscuits and butter.

Three sticky-faced boys zipped past me, garish liquid dripping off their fingers, their Popsicles melting faster than they could suck them back.

I recognized one boy by his scarred and withered hand, the result of falling into a cooking fire as a toddler. His father was Joseph, the men's ward's night orderly.

"*Apinun tru*," I called out.

The boy stopped running and turned towards me. "*Apinun*, Dokta.*"

"How's your papa?"

"Okay." He slurped the green liquid pooling in his good palm and jogged after his friends, who were kicking an empty can towards an open space across the street.

Inside the shop, the yeasty aroma of fresh bread unlocked memories of happy afternoons in my grandmother's kitchen. I pictured pine trees, rays of sunlight sparkling on a lake, and tongues of flame dancing inside the firebox of a cast-iron stove.

My eyes grew accustomed to the trade store's dim light and piles of treasure appeared. Crates of beer, boxes of sugar, and tins of powdered milk rose from the floor like stalagmites. Stacked cans of fish loomed in precarious towers. Shiny cooking pots teetered on massive burlap bags of polished rice. Patterned shirts and *laplaps* hung from ceiling hooks like dozens of giant bats.

The oven-fresh smell beckoned me deeper into the aisles of the cavern.

I plucked warm bread, brown eggs, and other sundries from the shelves and handed Henry a fan of kina notes. He didn't smile.

He barely lifted his narrow-eyed gaze from the horseracing magazine splayed on the counter.

Slipping his pencil behind one ear, he punched at the cash register.

Urgent squeals and the thump of footsteps echoed from the stairway leading to the rooms over the store where his family lived.

"How's the baby?" I asked.

"Cries a lot."

"He hasn't been sick, has he?"

"No. He's fine."

I remembered that baby's delivery well. A breech birth. With every contraction the mother squeezed out a string of oaths like I'd never heard before. But then her father was a sea captain.

"How old is he now?"

Henry glanced at his watch. "Three months, four days, eleven hours, and twenty-six minutes."

He took the pencil from behind his ear and returned to his magazine, his nose nearly touching the page. He studied pencilled figures in the margins, lips fluttering in mute concentration as I left.

Fifteen minutes later, I was back at my place watching wisps of steam rise from two hardboiled eggs in a mixing bowl on my kitchen counter. Someone knocked at the door.

"Come in," I sighed. "Door's open."

I mashed the eggs with a fork and added a generous dollop of creamy Miracle Whip. Two slices of fresh bread lay on a plate in front of me. Saliva poured over my tongue.

There was another knock, then a confident voice: "Dokta?"

"Yes, I'm just making my lunch. Come on in."

I tossed in some diced onion and garlic, sprinkled on some salt and pepper, then whipped the mixture a few times around the bowl and dumped it onto a thick slice of soft white bread.

The first sumptuous mouthful hit my long-deprived stomach. I opened the door for my visitor. "Oh, Father. *Apinun tru*. Do you want to come in?"

Father Schiermann backed away from the door and held his hands in front of his chest. "Sorry, I didn't intend to be disturbing your meal." Though he smiled with his lips and his softly crinkled eyelids, his German accent still bothered me. Every sentence made him sound like the bad guys in the war movies I'd been raised on. His trademark white shirt, dark pants, and brown plastic sandals with rugged soles accentuated his fitness. The edge of his folded purple stole peeked out of a trouser pocket. For him, for me, the watch never ended.

I took another satisfying chomp from my sandwich. The priest's face took on an urgent look that told me I'd have no time for leisurely nibbling.

"Something wrong, Father?"

He backed into the shade of my guava trees and wrinkled his sun-scorched nose at the smell of the egg and garlic concoction I held in my hands.

"To the children's ward this morning I brought twin boys. Not yet two years old. Their mother helps sometimes cleaning my church." He rubbed his brow. "They're very sick. High fever. They look like little skeletons."

"I'd better go and have a look."

I was already angry as I returned to the kitchen, grabbed my canvas satchel from the table, and washed down the last of my sandwich with a swig of warm Coke. But my anger had nothing to do with my interrupted lunch.

With each urgent step toward the children's ward, the blood pumped hotter in my veins. Striding beside me, Father Schiermann was buried in his thoughts too. There was no reason kids had to starve while the sea and the village gardens overflowed with food. The twins weren't the first living skeletons to arrive at Vunapope. By now I'd seen dozens.

Initially, I'd reckoned that worms or malaria enlarged their spleens and engorged their tummies. But their skinny thighs and brittle hair betrayed malnutrition in its worst form. Skin peeled, ankles swelled, and death stalked their tiny frames. In Africa, they called it kwashiorkor. At Vunapope, the nurses looked away in embarrassment when I pointed out the telltale signs.

Sister Pirmina often scoffed to me that New Guinea families fed their children only *kaukau*, a starchy sweet potato with limited food value.

"Once these children come off the breast, they become malnourished. That just belongs to it," she'd pronounce before pushing up her spectacles and going off in search of dusty corners that hapless students hadn't swept with proper care.

Kids in New Britain weren't just malnourished, they were starving. Some died in our hospital cribs. We bundled up each corpse and were hit immediately by the next distraction. Sister Pirmina by her dusty corners. I by patients in an endless queue.

"I left them in Room Three," said Father Schiermann.

He led me into a room I knew well. It was lined with two rows of whitewashed beds and cribs. From a wooden frame high on the end wall, his exposed heart impaled by a flaming torch, an image of Jesus beckoned with outstretched arms across the airless pall of old fish and dirty bedpans. How could such a symbol inspire and console anyone, much less a man as sensible as Father Schiermann?

We squeezed past a woman sitting on the floor breast-feeding an infant. She smiled. On her mat of woven leaves lay a tall thermos flask, a white enamel mug of milky tea, an aluminum pot of boiled rice, and an open can of mackerel. A whole fish had been hacked into chunks and stuffed into the tin – flesh, bones, and guts. Like so many others, this woman was camped in the ward, her food, dishes, and firewood wrapped in a homemade mat. In caring for her school-aged daughter, she prepared meals over the open fire of the common cookhouse, and slept beneath the sick child's bed at night. Her pillowcase, embroidered with flowers, pleaded: "May our love last forever and never die, Darling".

We stopped at a crib containing two infant boys clothed only in skimpy diapers improvised from the remnants of threadbare towels. They stared at the ceiling. Skinny arms and legs, thin as the handle on my frying pan, lay limp and motionless. Flies pitched and dived above their bloated bellies.

"Here they are," said Father Schiermann. "Simon and Jonah,

from Malabunga village. They were born here at Vunapope. Yes, it was Easter time. Just past eighteen months ago."

I leaned over the crib. One of the boys struggled to sit up. He extended his arms towards us and started to whimper, but was struck by a wet staccato of coughing. He pleaded with his arms and with his eyes, their gaze magnified by lengthy eyelashes.

"This is Simon," Father Schiermann said. "He always wants to be held. I know him by that bump of skin beside his ear."

Tears etched the grime on Simon's face. Yellow mucus oozed from his nose like candle wax. His listless twin looked identical, except for the skin peeling in large brown flakes off his chest and belly. Deadly kwashiorkor.

I pursed my lips to contain my anger.

"I told you they looked like skeletons – one with bad skin and the other, a bad cough," Father said. He took a deep breath, shook his head, and briefly closed his eyes. "I always knew they were small, but never like this. It's weeks since I am seeing them. Nalla, their mother, brought them to my church this morning when she came to sweep the sanctuary. She worried about their fever." He wiped his forehead with his handkerchief and looked about the room. "Where did she get to?"

He strode off in search of Nalla as I dug into my satchel for my stethoscope. I lowered the railing on the crib, whispered cooing sounds, and reached in. Instead of recoiling like almost every other toddler I'd ever examined, Simon thrust his arms around my neck, hooked his bony legs onto my hip, and nestled his cheek into my chest. Gobs of his nasal mucus soaked my shirt. He smelled of runny stools and rotting fruit, curiously acidic and sour. I was smitten by the urgency of his stranglehold and the warmth of his feverish body. I sensed something starting to glow inside me, an inkling of the spark that drives a father to protect his children, to stop at nothing when called to snatch them away from harm.

By the time Father Schiermann returned with Nalla, I'd discovered that both boys burned with fever and rattled with pneumonia. Simon clung to my hip and nuzzled my chest. The ember he'd set alight burned hot within me. Nalla, a barefoot Tolai woman who looked pained and exhausted, stared at me blandly when I explained that we would start with pills for malaria and injections for infection.

"But what about their malnutrition?" asked Father Schiermann. "These boys are starving, yah?"

The threat of overwhelming panic roiled within my gut. "Yes, Father. But I don't know what to do about it."

My mouth went dry. I clutched Simon more tightly to my chest. "I've tried to get the nurses to feed other malnourished kids but they refuse to do it. They start intravenous drips. They willingly dole out medicines. They change bandages all day long. But they will *not* put food into children's mouths."

I pointed to a crib in the far corner of the room. "A little girl died right there last week. She had puffy feet and flaky skin. Just like Jonah. The nurses didn't feed her and the parents had no idea what foods to prepare or how much to give. In the end, she just took sips of water."

"Let me provide the food for these boys," Father said. "It's no problem." He opened his arms, palms up. "Already for many years my home parish in Germany is sending money. For the poor, a fund. And if you tell Nalla what to feed them, I know she will do it."

He smiled and asked Nalla in Pidgin what the boys liked to eat. Rice? Bananas? Fish, maybe?

Nalla looked confused.

I shook my head. "It's more complicated than that," I said. "When children are really sick like Simon and Jonah, they need a diet that's easy to digest and has lots of protein and energy. And has just the right amounts of salt and fluid. It has to be carefully calculated. If it's not done right, they go into heart failure."

Jonah stirred in his crib, looked towards his mother, and screamed. Nalla picked him up, blew gently into his face, and stroked his bony cheeks.

"I have a booklet from East Africa that describes a formula for treating kids with serious malnutrition," I said. "But Sister Pirmina hasn't let me try it. She says we're a hospital, not a hotel. We're not in the business of providing food. Not even milk. It would cost too much."

Father coughed and rolled his eyes. "What things do you need for this formula? They are expensive, yah?"

"Mostly just milk powder, sugar, and cooking oil. And water, of course."

"All this fuss over a bit of milk and sugar?"

"It's five feedings a day. And must be given exactly as ordered."

"You get your little book, Dokta. I am telling Sister Pirmina to provide what you need and send me the bill."

A shudder shot through my shoulder blades. A few generous donors, even if they were from her homeland, wouldn't buy our way through Sister Pirmina's wall of scepticism. The only way to convince Sister Piranha of the merits of our program was to show her the formula in action. Of course, if it failed, she would be only too glad to flash her needle-sharp teeth and shut the program down with a satisfied grin.

I did have an ally, my co-conspirator in the pharmacy, the hunchbacked nun with the southern drawl and the mischievous giggle. "Father, could we do this through Sister Leora? She can accurately measure out the ingredients in the pharmacy."

"Good idea," he agreed. "You tell her to prepare for me a list for shopping. I am buying what's needed from Henry Chen in Kokopo. We can start today, yah?"

"But will we ever get Sister Pirmina on side? She's…"

"It's okay." He put his hand on my shoulder. "You leave Sister Pirmina to me."

That afternoon, I tracked down Veronika, the most senior student now on rotation in Children's Ward. Her support would be pivotal. We hustled over to the pharmacy where Sister Leora leaped at the prospect of a new venture. Together we adapted the East African recipe to suit our needs, being sure to include all the ingredients required for restoring vital body proteins to the muscles, blood, and internal organs.

In the quantities needed to make one litre of formula at a time, we combined folic acid and potassium chloride from the pharmacy with whole milk powder, sugar, and cooking oil from the trade store. Veronika watched in studious silence, her eyes intent beneath the inky chevrons tattooed on her forehead.

"I knew one day I'd have a good use for all them empty instant coffee jars I've been keepin'," Sister Leora grinned. She giggled and rubbed her gnarled hands together. "The lids are nice and tight – keeps ants outta the mixture 'til it's ready to be used."

Veronika's springy hair danced beneath her cap as she lifted and jiggled the first jar, admiring the gooey concoction of oil, powder, and fine crystals.

"Like those packets of dried-soup-mix," I said. "When it's time for a meal, just add warm water and stir."

"May we give it a name, Dokta?" Veronika asked. "How about *Vunapope Special Formula*? V-S-F for short."

The booklet said that based on their body weight, puny as it was, we should give Simon and Jonah half a cup of formula each, five times a day. Veronika and I carried four lots of mixture and a brand new one-litre plastic measuring jug to the children's ward. Nurses gawked at the bizarre-looking potion inside Nescafé jars.

"It is called *Vunapope Special Formula*. V-S-F," Veronika said, deliberately enunciating every syllable. "And it is *not* food." She caught my eye with a knowing look. "It is *medicine*."

"We're going to give it to the twins in Room Three," I said.

Veronika laid a clean tea towel on the counter for our first demonstration and brought over a kettle of boiled water, now cooled to lukewarm. We made a show of washing our hands in the stainless steel basin we kept for that purpose, then I dumped a pre-measured jarful of VSF mixture into our new plastic jug. Veronika slowly filled the jug with water up to the one-litre mark and methodically stirred away the lumps with a wooden spoon. She poured the twins' first measured dose into matching enamel mugs and led us into Room Three, the mugs perched on a tea tray.

After Veronika described to Nalla the purpose of the formula,

I handed Nalla a spoon and pointed towards the frothy mugs. She looked impassive, then shrugged and tisked. I flushed with irritation. Why the haughty attitude? She should be bloody-well grateful.

The moment he saw his mother lift the mug from the tray, Jonah backed into the far corner of the crib. When she approached him, mug and spoon in hand, he screamed like a siren. Nalla shook her head, plunked down the mug, and dropped the spoon onto the floor. The screaming stopped.

I picked up Simon and the other mug and spoon, and though he nuzzled close, he clamped his lips and pushed the spoon away with his scrawny hand.

Nalla stared quietly at her two grotesquely skinny boys. Tears welled in her dark eyes; she dabbed them with the billowy hem of her *meri-blouse*.

Veronika looked crestfallen. "Dokta, please. We *must* make them drink our V-S-F." She turned to Nalla and wagged her finger just like Sister Pirmina did when she was scolding. "Nalla, you have to be…"

"It's okay, Veronika," I said. "We can do this another way."

The handbook predicted the possibility of this setback. Malnutrition could make children so ill that their bellies ached, and painful sores lined their gums and throats. They just could not eat. Not even drink. I would have to feed each twin through a tube inserted into his nose, down the esophagus, and into his stomach.

The nurses rounded up the tubes and lubricating jelly. After a great deal of coughing, spluttering, and screaming, I managed to coax a feeding tube into Simon, then Jonah. The poor little guys looked sadder than ever with heavy strips of adhesive tape plastered across their cheeks.

Veronika retrieved a large syringe from a cupboard, filled it with VSF from Simon's mug, and pushed it slowly into the tube that dangled from his nose. I held him close, willing him not to vomit up his only chance for cure. We watched and waited in the still room. After a few moments I gave a nod. Veronika filled the syringe again and pushed its plunger. She pulled and pushed a few more times until she'd emptied the mug.

The formula stayed down. Every drop. Simon's light frame felt warm against my chest. And, I hoped, a little strengthened.

Nalla picked up Jonah and held him on her hip; Veronika repeated the routine.

In a few minutes, the twins lay side by side in their crib, fast asleep. Veronika beamed. My heart danced. Nalla sat down on the floor and stared at the image of Jesus high on the wall.

In the side office of the ward, Veronika found a blank sheet of paper on which we wrote out a schedule for feeding the twins. Exactly half a cup of VSF, five times a day. We made a place for the staff to sign when each dose was given, just like a medicine. No mistakes. No missed doses.

Veronika explained the procedure to the slack-jawed junior students who shuffled their feet and stared at the floor. I chuckled to myself at the sight of her admonishing finger.

"My classmate, Adelina, and I will return this evening," she promised. "We'll make sure the juniors give the V-S-F properly."

Each morning for the next three weeks I arose a few minutes early and made Simon's and Jonah's crib my first stop after breakfast. I rushed to read their bedside charts, to scrutinize each dose of VSF, each recorded weight, and every fever.

After a week, Jonah began to sip from his mug. Then Simon. We removed the feeding tubes.

My doctor's eye observed the malignant flakes on Jonah's skin give way to mottled smoothness and watched the cracks and sores on Simon's lips shrink and later heal; but my paternal eye marvelled at the light that crept into their faces, their widening smiles that morphed into laughter when I pulled silly faces, and the growing strength in Simon's eager hugs.

In the treatment room, I puffed with pride at the sight of two students stocking the cupboard with another load of VSF-filled coffee jars from Sister Leora. I was prouder still to watch from a corner while they scrupulously prepared a fresh litre of the formula. Such precision, shown by girls who'd emerged from villages that had never known a measuring device, made my heartbeat quicken.

Edwina, the Tolai nurse in charge of Children's Ward, had been away the week we launched the VSF. I'd left it to Veronika to tell her about our new program, being in no hurry to witness for myself her eyes flashing in silent but clear complaint that it all sounded like too much trouble.

After one of my morning calls on Nalla and the twins, Edwina directed me toward a schoolboy who had just arrived with a swollen knee. Edwina would turn this into another exasperating guessing game, just as she'd done when Oska presented his *pigbel*. She'd know all the details of the boy's story, but watch stone-faced at my struggle to tease out the specifics of his symptoms.

In the crowded room where my new patient lay covered in sweat, shivering with fever, I noticed a skinny toddler with bows in her hair, a feeding tube taped to her nose, and a mug by her bed.

I pointed to the girl. "What's this, Edwina?"

"Severe malnutrition."

The clipboard chart showed the girl's body weight dutifully recorded, her VSF doses accurately calculated, each feeding logged and initialled.

"Wow!" I was so delighted at this show of independence and initiative that I could make no pretence of restraining my enthusiasm, even in the presence of Edwina's heavy, passive gaze. "This is wonderful," I said, tapping at the neatly written figures on the chart. "Whose idea was it to start this girl on VSF?"

"Mine, Dokta," Edwina said.

"*Yours*?" I immediately regretted my incredulous tone. I'd misjudged her. Edwina was taciturn and stolid, but she wasn't indifferent. The heat in my cheeks signalled my embarrassment. Damn. "Are... Are... Her feedings. Are they staying down?"

Edwina nodded. When she picked up the mug and cracked the tiniest of smiles, I realized I'd crossed the hazardous shoals of doctoring and reached the hallowed shores of *Development*. I pictured the preachy mavens of CUSO, my sponsoring agency, in paper-cluttered offices, nodding their approval of my pilgrimage to that holy land where stopgaps are banned; where brown skins learn to keep mastering their problems long after paler mentors have retreated to spotless Switzerland, noble Norway, or cozy Canada.

Edwina coaxed a sip of VSF past the girl's raw lips and motioned to the mother to do the same. The child took two gulps and let out a burp. All my notions of mavens, brown skins, and stopgaps evaporated. Every bleary hour I'd spent in medical school digesting horse-choking textbooks, enduring desert-parching lectures, had led to this moment.

"Does Sister Pirmina know about this girl?" I asked. Sister had let it be known she disapproved of VSF, but never voiced her objections. I assumed Father Schiermann had been very convincing or pulled rank, King of Hearts trumping Queen of Spades.

"Yes," Edwina answered. "But Sister says she'll get malnourished again when she goes back home." Edwina peered into the crib and clucked softly. "Is that really going to happen?"

"We're going to make darn sure it doesn't. The same goes for Simon and Jonah. They'll be going home..." My throat tightened. I couldn't imagine mornings without Jonah's laugh and Simon's hugs. "We'll have to show mothers how to add extra calories and protein to their children's diets."

Humble versions of Henry Chen's store dotted the countryside wherever a small supply truck could negotiate the roads and tracks. "We'd better make a list of simple foods that people can buy in their local trade stores," I said. "Fatty foods for calories, and some meat or fish for protein. Nothing too expensive. Are eggs hard to find?"

"Not always."

"Let's include them as well. We'll send mothers home with simple instructions about better nutrition – preparing some foods from their gardens and others from the trade stores. How good are you at drawing pictures?"

Edwina looked down at her bare toes. Was there a hint of blushing on her nutmeg cheeks? "Let me ask the students."

7

Spirits

The knocking was distant and measured, yet insistent. I drifted groggily, effortlessly toward the sound.

A man's face loomed at a doorway. It bristled with beard and bad temper. "Dokta; she wants it back. You must give it back."

Tears glazed a young woman's bloated cheeks, her eyes bloodshot as she pleaded:. "Why did you take it away, Dokta? Please, put it back."

The man heaved his axe into the air.

I tried to retreat from the blade's lethal arc, but something gripped my exhausted body, trapping me.

A thing – long and heavy and wrapped in green towels – nestled itself in my arms.

Blood dripped into dark pools on the floor. A visceral storm surged through my belly.

More knocking. This time crisper and more insistent.

The man lunged, pressing his wolf-like face into mine.

His teeth grew to fangs, his mouth foamed with spittle. "Give my daughter back her leg. That one there!"

The man jabbed a hairy paw towards the green thing in my arms. "That leg you cut off with your saw."

The knocking gave way to banging. Loud and desperate.

In the twinkling that it took my mind to winnow away husks of dream from kernels of reality, I realized that someone was standing outside and pounding a fist against my kitchen door.

Now fully awake, sweaty, and consumed by a palpable dread, I whipped back the sheets, swung my legs over the side of my bed, and rubbed grits of sleep from my eyes.

The luminous hands of the alarm clock gestured silently in the darkness: quarter past five a.m.

Glass and wood muffled the voice that called through the door. "Dokta. *Wanpela man he bigpela sick.*" I recognized the deep tones of Joseph, the night watchman from the men's ward.

In the moments it took me to fumble with the lamp switch and shuffle into my flip-flops, yesterday's events played in my head like an action movie.

There had been a car crash on the road to Rabaul. Two people dead at the scene and a teenaged girl, who was carried barely conscious into our operating theatre.

Her left leg was a mangled mess, unrecognizable from ankle to thigh. Its fractured bones twisted through her bloodied flesh, a corkscrew ripping through rotten cork.

"Well, it's gotta come off, that's all there is to it," Jack Randall had said, standing in the operating theatre with his gnarled surgeon's hands perched on his hips.

"No point in fartin' around," Jack continued, "when there's not a snowball's chance in hell that lower extremity is ever gonna act like a leg again. Better get out the saw and take it off before gangereen sets in. Eh, Ross?"

I had never seen an amputation before, let alone performed one. I thought of old Hollywood Westerns, the American Civil War, the trenches of World War I.

I explained to the relatives what we were going to do, that we had no choice. They gaped in horror and nodded their consent.

I could sense the father recalculating the *brideprice* of his now devalued daughter, his eyes reflecting the lost bonanza of cash, pigs, and seashells he would have gained upon the marriage of a strong and fertile daughter. A groom would not pay much for a bride who hobbled on one leg.

Sister Nina soon had the girl under a comforting blanket of anaesthesia.

I fastened a tourniquet high in the groin, painted the thigh with germ-killing iodine, and wrapped the lower part of the leg in green towels.

Jack Randall guided me through the procedure from the first cuts of skin, to the tying-off of blood vessels, to the surrealistic severing of the thighbone with a length of sharp wire fitted with handles on each end.

Jack pulled the fleshy tissues away from the bone, as if stripping the peel from a banana, and told me to pass one end of the wire under the bare femur.

I pulled the wire taught between its handles and stared through Jack's heavy glasses into his rheumy eyes. Now what?

"Well, Ross... you gotta draw that wire through the bone with a nice, smooth rhythm."

I pulled lightly on one handle, then on the other, barely stroking the wire across the bone's undersurface.

"Don't be afraid of it, son," Jack implored. "Come on, now. Pull up with some good firm pressure. A seesaw motion. Bone cutting is no job for weak wrists."

I licked the salty sweat off my upper lip, tightened my grip on the handles, and pulled the Gigli saw's wire blade back and forth across the young woman's femur.

It made a raspy sound, like a backsaw grating through a bough of green spruce.

"That's better." A dry cough tumbled from Jack's throat. We both could smell the sweet musk of bone dust. "To tell you the truth," he confided, "I've always hated the smell."

The wire itself seemed to know what to do, cutting a neat kerf through the thighbone.

I reached my final stroke, and Jack called "Tim-burr!" as the far half of the femur thumped onto the table.

Disgusted by his jocularity, I felt awash in a turbid soup of fascination and repulsion, nausea and palpitations.

"We've gotta have plenty of working room for stitching up the stump," Jack advised. "Lift the leg off the table and put it over there on the counter." He pointed towards the Formica countertop beneath the windows, behind which a score of relatives pressed their faces against the screens and louvers.

"Gotta make the gal a nice neat stump for her wooden leg. Nothing worse than an incision with puckers and dog-ears."

I was amazed at the weight of the leg in my arms, like a log of maple firewood ready for splitting.

The relatives ogled and gasped as I laid it on the counter in front of them.

When I looked at the toes, still intact, and peeking from beneath the cotton wrapping, I nearly swooned with the realization of what we had done. I half-expected the toes to wiggle in assertion of their humanness, but they remained sadly inert.

The vision of the amputation lingered in my mind until a fresh interruption jolted me back to reality. Joseph called again through my kitchen door, "Sorry, Dokta. You coming? *Telefone i-bagarup.*"

Yes, my telephone was off the hook. The cat must have knocked it during the night. She had done it once before. "Be there in a second."

I opened the door to find Joseph looking like a scolded dog with doleful eyes and a downturned lip. His drooping shoulders exaggerated his lack of height.

As usual, he was wearing just a green tee shirt, dark shorts, and black flip-flops.

His permanent night shifts and lack of uniform made his hospital status uncertain. Was Joseph a nurse, an orderly, or an untrained security guard? No one had bothered to introduce us, and I'd never asked for fear of insulting him.

Sister Pirmina dismissed him with sharp sneers, as though he were an ignorant child, not a father of six who arrived at his post every night at ten o'clock. At an hour when most men in PNG were whooping it up or sleeping it off, Joseph was punctual and sober.

Although he didn't hand out pills or administer injections, he was my midnight guide who served up nuggets of lore I could never have discovered for myself.

Joseph's Pidgin was easy enough to understand, as long as he didn't mumble. He wasn't mumbling now. "Sorry, Dokta. *Wanpela man he longlong. Bigpela sick come-up long him. Man he no can catchim wind.*"

In his ward he had a man who was deranged, ill, and breathless. Joseph usually coped with problems all night without bothering the sisters or the doctors, so his presence at my door meant the patient had something unusual.

Joseph had said the man was *longlong*, which conjured visions of a crazy man swinging an axe inside the men's ward.

The man we encountered was certainly *longlong*, but not in any shape to swing an axe.

Splayed out on the floor between two rows of beds, and dressed only in a pair of torn shorts, he was thrashing like an exhausted swimmer making a frantic thrust for a distant shore.

We hoisted him off the floor and led him, flailing and raving, onto his bed.

His lips and tongue were pink, his pulse strong. He didn't have a fever and he didn't smell of booze. He was panting deeply, each breath whistling past his teeth.

Robust sounds rang from his heart and lungs through my stethoscope. His problem didn't lie within his chest.

The vacancy of his face alarmed me. His pupils loomed large and black and round, like a pair of hockey pucks. They didn't constrict when I aimed my flashlight into them.

At the back of each eye, the tissues were red and swollen, as though the retinas were on fire. Something had torched the cable of nerves connecting his eyes to his brain.

"Joseph," I queried, "he can't see?"

"Yes."

"Was he blind before?"

"No, Dokta. *Man he cuttim copra. He work long wanpela plantation*." He couldn't have been blind, not and make a living opening coconuts with a machete on a copra plantation.

Joseph was as puzzled as I was. "Why he sick, Dokta?"

"Don't know."

Malaria could cause delirium and fever, but not blindness. Likewise meningitis and brain abscess.

There was no indication that he'd been kicked or punched.

His unrelenting panting looked like the final stages of untreated diabetes, when excess acids in the bloodstream trigger a peculiar pattern of hyperactive breathing.

Three men, dressed in *laplaps* and grubby nylon shirts with the buttons missing, had been exchanging conspiratorial glances from the foot of the bed throughout my inspection of the patient.

Although the arrival of a sick newcomer was always a spectacle in the men's ward, these three had more than a passing interest in my patient. If he had diabetes, there would be sugar in his urine, and I could settle him with insulin shots. All I needed for the diagnosis were a few drops of urine.

I cajoled two of the men to bring their mate to his feet by gripping him under his armpits, but I couldn't get them to pull down his shorts, or grasp his wrinkled penis, or hold the white enamel urinal by its handle. Those finer points of urine collection were left to me.

With the man's shorts around his ankles like a camel's hobble, the four of us danced an awkward two-step in front of a wide-eyed crowd.

Sweating to keep both the patient and the urinal upright, I crouched to catch any drop of urine he might produce, his hairy genitals directly at my eye level. At long last, we heard a tinny tinkling followed by an unrestrained gush.

I carried the full container to the side room we used as a makeshift laboratory, sensing an uncomfortable intimacy with the steamy warm urine. Cold urine is just an anonymous specimen; warm urine is fresh and personal, and connects the doctor too directly with the patient who produced it.

Then, I plunked the brimming urinal down on the battered wooden desk, relieved that I hadn't slopped any urine on my bare fingers.

I sat on a stool and lit the spirit lamp on the desk. I poured a little of the urine into a test tube, dropped in a sugar-testing tablet, gripped the tube with a pair of tongs, and held it over the flame. The tablet fizzed and changed colour. Brick red would have signalled a positive result, but the urine turned a greenish blue. Negative. No sugar in the urine. No diabetes.

Now, I sat alone in the stuffy side room and gazed at the flickering flame of the spirit lamp, my brain searching through its index of medical conditions. Nothing came to mind.

The bright blue of the lamp fuel glistened in its glass reservoir beneath the flame. It reminded me of the other night at the golf club when the power had failed. Kent Eastman had brought out a container of meths from a back cupboard and refilled the lamps with bright blue fuel. Roger Hunter, the lascivious pharmacist, had said that village men get drunk on the lamp fuel when they run out of beer.

I recollected from a lecture in medical school something about methanol poisoning causing blindness, delirium, and panting respirations. What Canadians called methanol, Australians called meths.

Had my patient been drinking methanol? He was too *longlong* to make any sense, and I could hardly expect his three buddies to admit to me that anyone had consumed the clandestine hooch.

I blew out the lamp, returned to the bedside, and asked Joseph to worm the truth out of them.

Leaving him to it, I sat on the porch outside the ward and listened to the hatching sounds of the new Saturday. Roosters crowed a raucous counterpoint to a sweeter birdsong chorus. Dogs snapped.

Doors banged. A baby cried. Men coughed from the pits of their lungs, hauled phlegm through their raspy throats, and exploded it off their tongues.

Joseph's hushed conversation wafted through the louvers in disjointed phrases I could not understand. At long last he appeared, a solemn look on his face.

"Yes. Man he been drinkin' meths."

"Really? That's wonderful."

Joseph looked puzzled. "But Dokta, it's poison."

Joseph was right. My enthusiasm was gauche. The man had ingested a blinding dose of methanol and I was overjoyed to have correctly sleuthed it out.

I sobered my tone. "Do they know when he drank it?"

"Yesterday."

"Did he drink the spirit straight out of the bottle?"

"No. He boil it first."

Joseph described how village men boil the blue meths in a pan until the colour disappears. When the colour has gone, so have both the bitter taste and the poison.

I tried to imagine the chemistry at work when simple boiling turns poisonous methanol into regular drinking alcohol. It sounded too much like alchemy.

In the six months since I'd arrived at Vunapope, this was my first case that looked anything like methanol poisoning. Why had the meths poisoned this man but not hundreds of secret drinkers before him?

In the long shadows of daybreak, with the sun peeking through the treetops, I hurried to my office in the hospital's main quadrangle at the top of the driveway.

I unlocked the door, grabbed my black handbook from the bookshelf, and flipped to the chapter on methanol poisoning.

The authors wasted no ink on niceties. They explained that methanol, the key ingredient of methylated spirits, is extremely poisonous. Two teaspoons cause blindness and three can kill. It lingers in the body ten times longer than regular drinking alcohol.

The ill effects start a day or two after ingestion and result only after methanol has been slowly metabolized by the liver into toxic acids and formaldehyde. Yes, I had read correctly: The body transforms methanol into the principal ingredient of embalming fluid. No wonder death can occur after just one drink.

There was a little good news in the chapter. Methanol's degradation can be minimized, and the toxic effects mitigated, by the timely administration of drinking alcohol.

In other words, a chaser of vodka or whiskey, if given soon enough, is the antidote to methylated spirits.

And the book advised the use of bicarbonate of soda – the baker's staple – to neutralize the toxic acids that had incited my patient's frantic panting.

But there was also more bad news – a warning that success in treatment depends on kidney dialysis, a host of laboratory tests, and intensive care. Nowhere in PNG was there access to kidney dialysis or the advocated laboratory tests. The best I could offer was my Vunapope version of intensive care.

The man's outlook did look dismal, but by the time I had almost memorized the chapter on methanol, a familiar chorus of keys clicked and jangled in the lock of the pharmacy door a few steps away from my office.

If anyone could help me with this case, it would be Sister Leora. She could make up a potion for just about anything.

Sister greeted me with a big smile and a wave of crooked fingers. "Hi there! How ya doin' today, Doc? I've come in early to make another batch of that VSF. They're goin' through it faster than ice cream cones at a Sunday school picnic."

I explained that there was a man with methanol poisoning in the men's ward and I wanted to make up a solution of drinking alcohol to give him intravenously, as he was in no condition to swallow it.

Her eyes sparkled behind tiny wire spectacles. "They used to give mothers alcohol by I.V. to stop their premature labour. It did the trick, all right." She let out a laugh. "But I guess they stopped doin' it because the mothers got drunk and the babies came out tipsy."

She figured we could easily add drinking alcohol to our regular bottles of intravenous fluids. "I keep pure alcohol – under lock and key, mind you – for my famous cough syrup." She donned her blue gingham apron. "Everyone loves it."

We scoured the fine print of my handbook, searching vainly for instructions on dispensing alcohol by the intravenous route.

How much should we give and how fast should we give it? We didn't know and the handbook wouldn't tell us.

Sister's enthusiasm outstripped her familiarity with alcoholic cocktails, her sight for tiny print, and her skill at arithmetic, so it took many scribbled computations before we agreed on a mixture.

We decided to infuse every hour intravenously the same amount of alcohol that's contained in one stiff vodka-and-tonic. It was just a wild guess but it would have to do.

With a litre of our alcohol formulation in one hand and a bottle of bicarbonate in the other, I jogged down the hill to the men's ward, thinking I was well on my way to curing my patient.

At the entrance to the ward Sister Girhildis clucked like a hen that has discovered a snake in her barnyard. "Dokta. In my ward, five men I am having. Blind and panting. And completely *longlong*. They are wild. Tell me, vat is going on?"

Sister's eyes widened as I told her of the men's situation. Now, her white skirts fluttered and flapped as she strutted from room to room, scolding the stuporous men for what they'd brought upon themselves. She cackled that in all her twenty years with the mission, she had never seen anything like this.

As I walked past the beds and encountered one vacant face after another, the calamity of the situation hit me like a distillery delivery truck. It took some fast-talking to bring Sister down an octave and then convince her that my outrageous plan to give these men even more demon alcohol was based on sound science.

If we were going to save these five from death or permanent blindness, our treatment would have to be well-organized and carefully executed. The nursing care at Vunapope, though always well intentioned, was almost never meticulous. It was all very well for the handbook to prescribe a pedantic strategy dreamed up in Toronto, but my men's ward was three shabby cabins strewn across Robinson Crusoe's back yard.

I had no idea what would happen when we started our treatment. How could we give intensive-style therapy to agitated men who pulled out their needles and stumbled around the ward like cantankerous drunkards? Would my estimated doses of alcohol and bicarbonate fulfill their complicated requirements? Too much bicarbonate would kill them as readily as too little.

Numbers flustered the nurses and measurements befuddled them. But they'd made a success of the VSF, and my only choice was to count on them again. We put all the affected men into one cabin to create an intensive care unit; and for each patient we identified a buddy whose task was to restrain his mate while we carried out our treatment.

The greatest help came from Adelina, a senior nursing student from a village near the beach, and Veronika's best friend. An unflappable teenager with mahogany skin and short frizzy hair, she stretched her neat blue uniform to its limits with her buxom top and wide bottom. All day, she circulated like a bumblebee in a field of clover, counting respirations, measuring volumes in urinals, and checking the outflow from intravenous bottles.

She sent the aides up the hill to Sister Leora for bottle after bottle of I.V. alcohol and bicarbonate. More than once she hissed at her juniors when they dislodged an I.V. needle or didn't properly regulate the flow of an I.V. drip.

The alcohol proved to be an excellent sedative. Men who had been stumbling into walls and shouting incoherently, drifted off to sleep. I adjusted their infusion rates to keep them snoring breezily, but not in deep comas from which they might never emerge.

I judged each patient's need for bicarbonate by counting the rate of his respirations. When the rate of frantic puffing began to fall, I knew that the level of toxic acids –and the need for bicarbonate – was falling, too. At mid-morning, when the first man began to puff less rapidly, I was ecstatic with relief and ordered Adelina to slow down his bicarbonate lest we kill him with too much of it.

There was no time for gloating over our early success. Six more men stumbled into the ward, all in the same frightful condition as the others. Sister Girhildis flapped and cackled in despair. Adelina shuffled the beds in her unit and pressed on.

At one point, I watched Adelina arguing in Tolai dialect with a young man wearing the grubby shorts and frayed shirt of a plantation labourer. She was clearly angry. Or frightened. The fellow stomped out the door.

Adelina straightened her apron and approached me with heavy steps. "He's jealous," she said. "Doesn't like me working in the men's ward."

She avoided my eyes and spoke in a harsh whisper. "The idiot thinks I'm going to be his bride. My father thinks so too." She waved brusquely with her large hands. "They can both forget it."

Jack Randall came down to the men's ward about midday. "You've really got a circus on your hands here, eh?" he said. "Well, I'm just a surgeon. I can only cure if I can cut." He chuckled at the old joke. "Basically, I know nothing about poisons. But it sure looks to me like you've gotten things here sorted out okay. I'll pinch-hit for you in Paediatrics and Maternity. It's kinda alien turf for me, but the sisters will keep me off the foul line."

In the early afternoon, half a dozen healthy-looking men turned up saying that they, too, had been drinking meths. They'd heard about others who'd been poisoned – two men had just died in their village.

The handbook underlined that the toxic effects of methanol are delayed for a day or two. Given the shocking state of the eleven men already under our care, I felt obliged to play it safe with these scruffy newcomers and provide them with the preventative antidote – hourly doses of drinking alcohol taken by mouth. Medicinal cocktails.

I returned to the pharmacy for a pow-wow with Sister Leora. She'd sent word that her pharmacy was closed to everything but the preparation of infusions for the crisis.

"How's it going, Sister?" I asked. "Right now, you must be the busiest bartender in all of New Britain."

Her face was flushed and her manner more impish than ever. The intoxicating fumes of countless flagons had gone to her head. "I haven't had this much fun since the big feast we put on when John the Twenty-third – I mean the late Holy Father, God rest his soul - became pope. I worked the bar then, too."

I explained that we needed to serve cocktails to the still-healthy newcomers so they wouldn't go blind.

"Sure, Doc. We can spike Sister Assumpta's lemonade for the fellas." She let out a squeak of delight and wiped the sweat from her cheeks with the back of her hand. "Doc Randall's been helping me measure out the alcohol – them jugs feel mighty heavy after awhile. Mind you, his arthritis isn't much better than mine."

She threw me a wink and a grin. "I bet Sister Girhildis is mad about missing her precious afternoon nap."

Healthy-looking ruffians were soon gulping Sister Leora's hard lemonade, while smoking and kibitzing in the shade of the mango trees. They got mildly drunk in a pleasant sort of way and must have been titillated by the sight of the venerable Sister Girhildis and her prissy student nurses serving them endless rounds of free drinks.

With their inhibitions diminished, a couple of the men strummed their guitars while others took out their betel nuts and chewed them in plain sight. If it were not for the hourly cocktails, they would never have risked the inevitable tongue lashing from Sister Girhildis, who was known to squawk at the copious and indiscriminate spitting of the betel nut ritual.

More men arrived who claimed a need for our mirthful remedy, but we kept things nicely under control until yokels began arriving by the truckload.

The word had got out that we were serving booze on the lawns of Vunapope Hospital to practically anyone who wanted it. Before we realized what was happening, lines of vans and pickup trucks were stretched along both sides of the hospital drive. The stencilled names of cocoa and coconut co-operatives, from villages all over the region, boasted from the side panels. By late afternoon, some three hundred rowdy men crowded the grounds of the men's ward. Red and yellow petals littered the walkways – the trampled remains of Sister Girhildis's prized cannalillies.

Men jumped through the croton hedges, casting in their wake broken clusters of shiny green and yellow leaves.

Roughnecks jostled in competition for the attentions of two prim but flustered nurses stationed at an impromptu triage desk, writing names in a logbook.

The men in the growing horde appeared perfectly well. How many were telling the truth and actually had drunk methylated spirits within the past couple of days, we had no idea.

I did know that we could not serve medicinal martinis, hour after hour, to every adult male within driving distance of Vunapope. With one third of the beds in the men's ward occupied by dangerously poisoned men – the number had mushroomed to sixteen – our resources were taxed to the breaking point.

It was clear that despite the risks of refusing to give prophylactic alcohol to the few who really needed it, we had no choice but to terminate our preventative program. The nuns of Vunapope could not provide an open bar to all of East New Britain.

Sister Pirmina, the matron, was relieved at my decision. Her patience was exhausted, especially as men began to trade insults and punches in the lengthening shadows of the late afternoon.

She stood on a wooden box, thrust forward her bosom, and appealed in her most authoritative voice for everyone to get back into their trucks and go home.

Few could hear her above the din of revving engines, slamming doors, and general raillery. Anyone who did was enjoying the camaraderie too much to pay attention.

Eventually, Sister called the police. They arrived in a couple of trucks just at nightfall and managed to disperse the crowd with surprisingly little effort.

The men must have realized that a promise of unlimited drinks at the mission was a far-fetched fantasy and there was no point in provoking the billy clubs of the local constabulary.

It was late in the evening before the situation began to settle down inside the men's ward. Adelina was still at work, checking her infusion rates.

Her nurse's cap was missing, and her once crisp white apron was wrinkled and grimy, but she beamed at the progress of the sixteen patients under her care. There'd been no further interference from her jealous boyfriend.

I'd taken time for nothing but a few guzzles of soft lemonade since Joseph had banged on my door those many hours ago. When Sister Pirmina sent chips and grilled lamb-chops for the men's ward staff, I wolfed mine down in four gulps.

At midnight, I dragged myself up the hill for a cursory tour of the maternity and paediatric bungalows. Mercifully, no labouring woman required my attention, and the kids were safe enough in their beds. I shuffled home and dropped onto my bed without the energy to take off my clothes.

Compared with Saturday, Sunday was a church picnic. No crowds clamoured at our doors. The typhoon of poisonings blew away as abruptly as it had roared in.

We had time to ask the obvious question: why did so many men from all over the region become poisoned with methanol at the same time? There must have been a common link, but not a single fellow would divulge the nature of his drinking escapades.

The nurses whispered that an enraged Tumbuan had caused wicked or foolish men to lose both their minds and their eyesight. The Tumbuan was merely a name to me. To the Tolai people he was a powerful spirit that filled them with terror.

At week's end, we completed our tally of the damage. We had admitted eighteen men in critical condition. All regained their mental faculties, but eight were permanently blinded. We had served spiked lemonade to 194 villagers who looked healthy, but claimed they'd been poisoned.

Not one man had died under our care.

We got word from Nonga, Rabaul's government hospital, that

about a hundred men had crowded their emergency department that Saturday. Fourteen had died there.

Two Saturdays later, Dr. Angus Macallan slipped through the door ahead of me at the *Café de Paris* in Rabaul. Angus was the chief of staff at Nonga. Most weeks I attended his clinical seminars where we traded interesting cases, and he dispensed pearls from his encyclopedic knowledge of Tropical Medicine.

The grey skies and drizzle of his Scottish childhood, still reflected in the wrinkles of his face, had sapped any sparkle he might ever have had in his gait or his voice.

But today he was ashen. His hand trembled on the doorknob. He nodded at me briskly. "Hello, Ross."

"Hello, Angus. Are you okay? You look like you could use more than a coffee."

He lifted his eyebrows and pointed towards an empty table in the far corner.

We ordered two cappuccinos. While the espresso machine thundered and fumed, he pulled a folded handkerchief from his pocket and wiped the sweat from his face – right cheek, left cheek, brow, chin. He smoothed the hanky with both hands and placed it on the table. He looked ready to speak, but stopped short when the waiter pranced over with two foaming cups.

Angus took a long draught of his coffee and swept the room with his gaze. "I've just come from the morgue at Nonga. Mother of God, it was hot in there. I must still smell of blood and formaldehyde."

"The cool air in here is a real treat, isn't?" I said. "The only place you can sit down and feel half-way normal."

He lifted his hanky from the table and dabbed the foam from his upper lip. "The police were there. And the magistrate – now there's someone with no stomach for post mortems. Fainted cold on the floor when she saw who it was on the table."

"Was someone killed?"

"Aye, Roger Hunter."

Unavoidably a memory of Roger's oversize penis flashed

through my mind. "The pharmacist," I said out loud. "What happened?"

Angus leaned into the table and lowered his voice. "He was murdered. Bashed on the head, then sliced open with a machete – throat to belly."

I felt the blood run out of my cheeks. My cappuccino tasted bitter and it churned in my stomach. "What happened?"

"*Payback.*"

"What?"

"*Payback*. You know, an eye for an eye. Native justice, PNG-style. Roger sold a new batch of meths – a few men died, more went blind. So they broke into his house, and.... and mutilated him."

"But they'd known all along not to drink the meths without first boiling out the blue colour. They knew it was poisonous."

"Actually, Ross... the blue stuff was never poisonous. It didn't contain methanol. Just regular alcohol and a harmless blue dye to make it taste bitter."

Joseph didn't have his chemistry straight, but he'd been more or less correct: the "meths" they boiled and drank in the villages was safe. The truth was, it had always been safe, even before boiling; it had never really been meths at all – more like industrial vodka with a bitter taste and a strange colour that could be removed by heating.

Angus twiddled the gold signet ring on his little finger. It was much like my own. "Selling real methanol has always been illegal in PNG because it's well-known that men drink whatever type of spirit is sold as lamp fuel."

"So, what happened two weeks ago?"

"Roger ran out of blue meths. He purchased a barrel of pure methanol from the paint factory. They use it in their plant. He sold that in small bottles – strictly as lamp fuel. It burns perfectly well."

"But he knew they would drink it."

"Yes," Angus agreed.

"Jesus," I muttered. There'd been nothing mystical about the methanol poisonings. No Tumbuan shaman. No alchemy gone wrong. Just groups of men drinking together as they did every weekend.

But this time they'd been sold a modern spirit that was pure poison.

In the awkward silence, Angus picked up his paper serviette and rubbed at stray drops of coffee on the tabletop.

I toyed with the foam on my cappuccino. An unanswered question hovered like a vulture. Why had there been fourteen methanol deaths at Nonga on that crisis weekend, but none at Vunapope? We'd faced equal numbers of serious cases.

"That was quite a weekend, eh Angus?" I was doing my best to sound casual. "Never seen anything like it before. At first, I had no idea what to do." I licked the froth off my spoon. "What strengths of I.V. alcohol and bicarb did you guys use?"

"Ach, Ross. The men had brought it on themselves. We didn't give them alcohol or bicarbonate."

"You didn't treat them?"

"Well, not as such. It would have been impossible to arrange, especially on a Saturday."

Dumbfounded, I stared at him in mute disbelief. *You just let the poison do its work? You let fourteen men die?* It was an effort not to say the words out loud.

"In any case," he continued, "we couldn't find our dispensary technician. Drunk or hung-over in his village, I expect. And no one else can unlock the pharmacy. Against hospital policy..." He coughed and looked around the café.

Hospital policy? Wordlessly, I signalled for my bill. I paid and left without saying anything further.

As I walked out, Angus was massaging his temple and staring into his coffee cup, looking anywhere except at me.

I imagine he avoided mirrors for a while, too.

8

Mud, Medicine and Magic

Rain surged from the sky for five days without a pause.

The stacks of clouds became so thick that at noon the equatorial sun could muster only feeble twilight.

The immaculate lawns and flowerbeds of Catholic Mission Vunapope lay inert, flat, and grey. Gone were the brightly dressed women, lingering under mango trees, laughing and confiding over their mending and embroidery. The hospital's doorways framed glum, brown faces mesmerized by the raindrops that crashed onto puddles and bounced like leaden fireworks. There was no escape from the roar of the torrents pummelling the tin roofs above us.

Indoors, humidity pervaded everything. I fell asleep between clammy sheets, and each morning my underwear, though recently laundered, felt soggy, and the waistband cold against my skin. My leather belt, my shoes, my camera-case lurked in the closet under layers of fuzzy mould that grew thicker by the hour.

The pervasive odour of damp soil conjured memories of hide-and-seek played behind boxes and cobwebs in the dark corners of my grandmother's basement.

On the afternoon of the sixth day, the rain ceased. The clouds cleared and the searing sun returned in full force. Steam rose from the grass, the tarmac, the rooftops. Vivid reds and yellows returned to Sister Girhildis's cannalillies, now rehabilitated after their violation by the rowdy hordes of the methanol crisis. Laughter echoed from every leafy, shiny corner of the mission.

I finished my workday in the women's ward and strolled down the avenue to my house, delighting in the swirls of saffron, violet, and mercury in the sky at dusk. My plan was to scare up a quick supper, update my diary, and write a few letters.

In the absence of convenient or affordable international telephone service, light blue aerograms, tissue-thin but heavy with news, travelled a six-week circuit across the Pacific. Home to Canada and back. I tried my best to sustain the rhythm of my longhand conversations with distant friends and family, but many evenings pulled me into crises in the operating theatre or left me too exhausted to pick up a pen. Today, I felt energized by the lifting of the storm clouds and prayed for an hour or two of détente in the emergency department.

Tucked next to the stethoscope in my satchel lay a mail-packet bonanza. Six unopened envelopes. I could almost hear the aerograms calling me to hurry home and peel back their flaps. Did one of them carry further details of the snags in my sister's plans to marry Harvey, her choleric stockbroker? Had Cousin Honoria yet delivered her triplets? And which boyfriend did they look like, the Jamaican banker or the Singaporean cellist? I decided to prolong the enjoyment by waiting until after dinner to savour the contents of each handwritten page.

I got only halfway through a plate of reef fish and boiled sweet potato when the phone blared its shrill summons. I pressed the receiver hard against my ear and strained to make out the muffled mumbling of Joseph, the bashful orderly in the men's ward.*

"Wanpela man i-stop. Bel belong him i-pain." Joseph had a man on the ward with pain in his belly.

I pressed him for details. "Does he look sick?"

"Yes." A cacophony of coughing, retching, and spitting could

104

be heard in the background. "You coming, Dokta?"

"Sure, Joseph. I'll be there soon."

I thumped down the receiver, finished off my dinner, and let out a tired sigh as I eyed the neat stack of aerograms still unopened on the counter. Battalions of ants, marching in linear formation, were hauling the breadcrumbs from my breakfast plate. Reinforcements would soon work on the remnants of my supper. I flicked off the light and slipped into the night, knowing a family of cockroaches would soon scurry from their hiding places to feast on the bits of onion and potato on the floor. At least they had no interest in the aerograms.

Joseph was waiting for me at the door of one of the men's ward bungalows. Deep furrows creased his brow.

He pointed across the room towards one of ten beds lined up in two rows. "The sick boy he over there," he said. "That big man, he got blue *laplap*, he papa belong him."

With massive arms folded across his chest and bare feet splayed firmly on the concrete floor, the not yet middle-aged father stood guard beside his son. The bulky metal bracelet of his Japanese watch flashed above his wrist. Whorls of black stubble peppered his dark cheeks and smears of mud slashed his tee shirt. Securing his blue paisley *laplap* was a wide leather belt, buckled by a chrome-plated bison's head. He gripped the keys to his pickup truck, and under one arm clutched an oddly dainty purse, woven at home from coconut fronds. When he opened the purse to put away the keys, I saw his cigarettes, a handful of smooth green betel nuts the size of crab apples, caustic lime powder wrapped in a banana leaf envelope, and a cluster of wrinkled pepper pods each the size of a green bean. The man's front teeth loomed like black daggers, stained by the mildly intoxicating and powerfully addictive betel nuts he chewed. His breath was hot with the bite of ginger and the pungency of liquorice. His lips and tongue, floridly reddened by betel pulp mixed with caustic lime, gaped like a fresh wound.

He acknowledged my approach with a quick lifting of the eyebrows – a PNG gesture I had come to realize meant either *yes, hello,* or *watch-out.* He turned his head and spat a blood-red jet of

105

betel and saliva precisely through the louvers of the window beside us, then turned back to study me like a coyote eyeing the throat of a tempting lamb.

The patient, lying passively on the bed, had the sparse and fuzzy whiskers of a youth not yet twenty. His face spoke of fatigue, fear, and pain, but he barely grunted in response to my questions. I asked if the bumpy truck ride to the hospital caused him *bigpela pain* – lots of pain. His father nodded in agreement.

The eyes of the youth widened when my enquiring hand hovered above the lower right part of his abdomen. He groaned when my fingertips confirmed the exact location of his pain and tenderness. Joseph had been correct. This case couldn't wait until morning. The boy had to have an operation as soon as possible. An appendectomy. His inflamed appendix was about to rupture. At any moment, it would burst forth its pus and overwhelm his belly with life-threatening putrefaction.

Dr. Jack Randall, our only surgeon, was away on a month-long holiday with his wife. Again, I was the only doctor at Vunapope. Dr. Hamilton, the surgeon at Nonga hospital, would have to do this boy's appendectomy.

I turned to Joseph. "We'll send him to Rabaul. Tonight." The ambulance trip would take about an hour in our aged four-wheel-drive vehicle. "Can you get someone to find the driver, Joseph? He lives nearby, right?"

"Road it *bagarup*." Joseph's eyes were downcast, as though it was his fault the highway was buggered-up – closed due to a landslide. Damn. The enormous volume of water dumped by the storm over the past few days had turned rich garden loam into greasy muck that tumbled down the hillsides. A muddy avalanche of bamboo trunks and uprooted bananas had obliterated our only link with Nonga Hospital and the town of Rabaul.

There was no way of getting this boy to a surgeon, and he needed his appendix removed as soon as possible. With the road impassable, the operation would have to be done at Vunapope. My pulse quickened in my throat. It looked like it would be up to me to operate. I looked again at his father. He was surveying my scrawny frame like a professional wrestler. Nausea gripped my stomach like a giant's fist.

It takes five years of training to fully cultivate the mystique required of a general surgeon, the medical magician who can handle and repair vital organs while a patient lies in a trusting sleep. Surgeons are educated within a hierarchy of military proportion, with clear-cut roles for trainees at every level. For the first two years, a young doctor is permitted only to steady the retractors – metal things that look like hand-held gardening tools – that keep the edges of the incision apart while the surgeon performs the elements of the procedure that require skill and talent.

The absent Dr. Randall was a real surgeon, of course. He was pleased to have me assist him at every operation, to help with the trickier parts when his eyesight proved insufficient. For me – as it would have been for any young doctor – this was the great thing about Vunapope. I held the scalpel right from the start without having to spend my junior years holding only the retractors. Under the watchful but cataract-clouded eyes of my mentor, I had removed the cysts of diseased ovaries, delivered babies by caesarean section, and performed appendectomies.

Now it appeared I was going to get to fly solo. I was going to cut open a young man's abdomen on my own for the first time. I trembled with excitement.

But of course I lacked the magic of a real surgeon. What would the nuns think about me tackling this case without Jack Randall?

I decided to ask the sensible Sister Nina, the nun who was the nurse-anaesthetist in charge of the operating theatre. If she had no objections...

On my third attempt to locate her by telephone, she came on the line. Yes, she was aware that the road to Rabaul was *bagarup*.

"I phone nurses now. In half-an-hour everything ready we will make." Her deep voice and German syntax were more noticeable over the telephone. "Theresa Lamoi will scrub. She knows all the instruments and at assisting she is quite good."

A haze of fear settled over my excitement. There were good reasons it took five years to become a surgeon, and if I buggered up it wasn't me who'd pay the price on the operating table.

Half-an-hour later, I was standing in the theatre at the simple basin where we washed our hands before surgery. I turned on the single tap and was reminded of the first time I'd tried to scrub-in on a surgical case, as a medical student back in Kingston, Ontario. It had taken forever because I was so nervous that twice I dropped the special nailbrush. At the end of the process I touched the tap with my scrubbed hand. I should have pushed the enormous wing-shaped handle with my elbow, not with my carefully sterilised fingers. A sharp-eyed nurse noticed my *faux pas* and was quick to scold. She insisted that the routine be started all over again. By the time I finally made it into the operating room, the surgeon was removing his gloves. The procedure was over.

I washed my hands now with a bar of ordinary soap and cold water. I didn't drop the nailbrush. The taps at the sink didn't have fancy handles, and a nursing student turned off the water after I finished scrubbing. No one scolded me.

Theresa, the teenage Papuan nurse who was doing an apprenticeship in the operating theatre, helped me into my sterile gown and gloves. Her movements were slow and tentative. Sister Nina observed, ready to pounce at any breech of our sterile technique. As a special favour, Sister had told Theresa to fit me out with a brand new pair of surgeon's gloves. I was pleased: The recycled and often-repaired gloves we usually wore made it awkward to handle instruments. Bulky homemade rubber patches covered the punctures and were invariably glued to the fingertips where they impeded delicate touch where it was needed most.

Standing over the anaesthetised youth with my scalpel poised above the abdomen, I fussed about the exact location of the intended incision and fidgeted with the sterile drapes of green cotton that covered most of the patient, except for a generous window of bare skin on the right half of his abdomen.

Just a few steps away, a crowd of relatives peered and muttered through the theatre's windows. The face of our patient's father, scrutinizing through the louvers, tempered my already shaky confidence. Conferring with an equally ferocious companion, he held up his huge hand and pointed in my direction. Nausea rolled through my stomach on waves of bile and butterflies. Were the father and uncle fascinated by the scene before them, or were they plotting their revenge – their *payback* – in the event the operation failed and the boy died? I couldn't help thinking about Roger Hunter: mutilated and shipped home to Australia in a wood casket.

I inspected the scalpel, held it tightly, and made a decisive cut through the boy's thick dark skin. Fat, muscle, and spurts of blood welled into the incision. With a final stroke, the blade entered the abdominal cavity over the appendix's usual resting-place. I was sailing solo on an open sea.

Usually, the appendix pops up like a worm right in front of you after you've slipped a groping finger into the belly. You tighten two loops of black silk thread around its base, as if to strangle a diseased grub, and you tie a few strategic knots. Then, snip-snip with the surgical scissors, and you're done. This appendix, however, was nowhere to be seen.

Theresa had set up the instruments in perfect order. She knew all their names, but never before had she held the retractors. She struggled with them. Several times they slipped out of her hands and the wound folded in on us, each time forcing me to reposition the instruments all over again.

When the retractors slipped for the fifth time within as many minutes, a string of swear words burst from my lips. Theresa looked down and away, her eyes conveying hurt and resentment. While my cheeks and ears burned with embarrassment, I slowed down my speech to phrases of exaggerated control, reinserted the retractors, and started hunting again.

I looked over to Sister Nina where she was standing at the young man's head, counting his carotid pulse under her fingers, and checking the colour of his lips.

I swallowed hard, then asked: "How's he doing, Sister?"

"He is stable, Dokta. He's a strong boy. Don't worry, I am having here everything under control."

I, however, began to fear that I would not get my part under control. The realization that I might never find the appendix triggered a wave of dread – an electrical storm that sparked at my toes, shot up through my legs, and ignited a forest fire in my chest.

My mouth held the bitter ashes of shame. It had been a mistake to take on this operation by myself. I'd wanted to be a hotshot. And now the boy was going to die. I could have tried treating him with antibiotics until the road to Rabaul had become passable – and I should have, no matter how many days it took.

A train rumbled past the door of the operating theatre, and a wind hissed through the coconut fronds beyond the windows. But, how could there be a train? PNG had no railways. No eighteen-wheelers either. The floor shuddered and bucked. The table stomped its legs like an angry adolescent, each bang of metal on concrete a terrifying jolt. The rumble became a growl, a roar. A monster, trapped beneath us, was hammering to get free.

I looked at Sister Nina for reassurance.

She shrugged.

Assorted objects in open cupboards thumped and clanged onto the floor, as if pushed by careless unseen hands. The clapboard walls swayed precariously. Our patient's relatives screeched and darted from their post at the window, like a flock of starlings scattered by gunshot. We were alone. My fear escalated. The fire in my chest raged out of control.

"It's only a *guria*," said Sister Nina. "At Vunapope, we are often having them."

I had never experienced an earthquake but could envision the floor gaping, the walls buckling, the roof crashing in. What was I supposed to do? Run for cover? What about the patient lying exposed on the table, paralyzed by anaesthesia, a wound yawning in his abdomen?

"What now, Sister?" I shouted above the din. I tossed the forceps onto the sterile drapes and ducked to avoid the wild swaying of the operating-lamp, which was suspended from the ceiling. It was a pendulum gone berserk at the end of its cord.

"Just stay where you are," Sister Nina replied. "The *guria* shortly will be over." There was a glint in her eye that told of the amusement she felt at seeing me experience my first earthquake.

The floor undulated under my feet, a rowboat hit by the wake of a passing freighter. Through the sterile drapes, I clung to the patient's flank, fearing I'd be pitched onto the floor.

Across the table, Theresa was clinging too. Her nutmeg face was obscured by her surgical mask and cap. All I could see were her eyes – a doe in a frozen moment of panic.

Ninety seconds later, the shuddering stopped, the roaring ceased, and the window-rattling settled. The crickets withheld their chirring. Silence hung like fog over a flat sea. The lamp swung in diminishing lazy circles like an osprey and returned to its perch above the table.

I was still gripping the torso of the youth, as if clutching the gunwales of a lifeboat, when Sister Nina chuckled. "Over is the *guria*, Dokta. The operation you can finish now."

I released my grip.

Two retractors had slipped out of the wound and lay scattered on the drapes with the other instruments we had tossed aside. A third retractor, a small rake with six curved fingers, was still deep inside the incision. It was askew, so I grabbed the handle to lift and reposition it. It wouldn't give.

Again I pulled on the handle, but the tines would not release the flesh caught in their grasp. I aimed the operating-lamp into the wound for a better look. A broad fold of tissue at the bottom of the wound had become tangled in the fingers of the instrument.

The quaking had twisted the retractor into the flesh, like a screwdriver. If I yanked roughly on the instrument, it would puncture the bowel with its sharp tines. Feces would spill out, and a simple incision would become a nightmare of excrement and microorganisms.

"This retractor is stuck, Theresa. Pass me the curved scissors."

With the scissors, I nibbled the tangled tissue away from the fingers of the rake. Trickles of sweat tickled my brow and rolled

111

down the back of my neck. I freed the tines one by one and delivered the instrument out of the wound like a newborn baby. Theresa dabbed the area with a cotton sponge, and I peered into the depths, desperately hoping I hadn't nipped the bowel or other vital structures. The intestine was intact. A broad band of fibrous tissue was in shreds and gave way to the pressure of my prodding fingers. With the separation of that fibrous tether, a large loop of bowel rolled to one side like a lazy sea lion. Peeking from beneath it was its pup, the appendix.

The boy had what surgeons call a retrocecal appendix, the most difficult kind to find and remove. Having stumbled upon it, I was back in control and smiling behind my mask. With an emotional rush of confidence, I probed and snipped with the scissors, dissecting the inflamed and bloated appendix away from the matted tissues that surrounded it. It was like removing the reluctant peel from a too-green banana. When the base of the elusive appendage came into view, I lassoed it with black cord and strangled its blood supply, then cut it free and held it high—like a prize catch—for everyone to see. It looked like a giant slug with rough red skin, but was still intact; it hadn't released its noxious pus. Theresa, her eyes smiling again, raised her enamel basin in a final step to land our trophy.

What a relief it was to close the incision and secure the last suture in the young man's skin. I looked over my shoulder. The expectant faces were again peering through the windows.

"*Mipela i-pinis. Him i-orait,*" I called out, affirming that the operation was all finished and the boy would be all right. The bravado was as much to reassure myself as the relatives.

The betel-chewing father gave a bright red grin, which no longer appeared ferocious. There was sparkle in his eyes, and the whites flashed in his brown face. He reckoned I had a touch of the surgeon's magic.

9

Partners

It was Dawna Wallis's turn to open the bidding.

I smiled, caught up in the enjoyment of an evening of playing cards with friends.

Janet Lundquist and I were up one game to none on a second rubber, having already won the first.

And Garnet Wallis didn't like losing at bridge, especially in his own kitchen.

As teachers at the Kokopo high school, Garnet and Dawna were entitled to a wood-frame house.

The place, a detached bungalow perched on head-high stilts above the mud and vermin, had the same layout as almost every house built for expats in government service: a front room that served as kitchen and living room, a tiny bathroom, and two small bedrooms separated by flimsy plywood walls.

I looked at the Spartan furnishings and once again felt comforted by the non-acquisitive lifestyle we shared.

We volunteers delighted in our simple life – homemade decorations, mismatched dishes, and few electrical gizmos – and we wore our self-satisfaction like an undervest of smugness.

There were times when we laughed in deprecation when letters from Home described how friends had special-ordered a dining-room suite, scoured the shopping malls for the perfect curtain fabric, or agonized over the tones of taupe latex when painting their bedroom walls.

In Kokopo, almost no one even had a phone. I had one to connect my house with the wards and switchboard of the hospital. When the outside line wasn't dead, I could be patched through to Rabaul, but no farther.

Dawna studied the thirteen cards in her hand. "I bid one diamond," she said. There was always optimism in her voice, whether she was contemplating her drive from the first tee, or facing a sink full of dirty dishes at the end of a Thursday-evening supper at Kokopo Golf Club.

"One heart?" Janet suggested questioningly with little conviction. She was new to the game and a tentative bidder. Having been a science major at university, and now Vunapope's lively laboratory technologist, she had a good head for figures. Trusting her instincts was paying off tonight.

"I pass," said Garnet. He'd been aptly named. After a beer or two, his cheeks glowed pink above his auburn beard. "Someone else must've cornered the market on good cards. They're sure not turning up in my hands."

Garnet pushed away from the table and headed towards the refrigerator. "Anyone want a beer?"

A fistful of royalty was staring at me, and I didn't care how pleased that made me sound. "I'm bidding three hearts. And no beer."

"We're having freshly baked pineapple upside-down cake and Milo at the end of this hand," said Dawna. "Garnet, if you have any more beer you won't be able to keep track of your cards."

Garnet flipped the cap off a bottle of South Pacific Lager. "I haven't gotten any cards worth keeping track of anyways."

Dawna took another look at what was fanned out in front of her. "I pass – on this hand and on the beer."

It was Janet's turn again. "Mm-mm, Milo. Don't you just *love* Milo? It's real delicious. We never had it in Minnesota, but my Aussie housemates and I have it practically every night. After supper. But why do they call it Milo? Isn't it just hot chocolate powder?" With a shrug and a broad smile, she announced her bid: "What the hay! Four hearts."

I was coming to delight in the sparkle in her eyes and in the lightness of her voice, including its flat, midwestern vowels.

Garnet, now leaning against the refrigerator, took a swig from his bottle. "Pass."

The cards in my palms guaranteed that Janet and I would win our second rubber with this hand. There was no need push it. "Let's leave it at four hearts. I pass, too."

Life didn't get much better than this. An evening with simpatico friends. Handfuls of winning cards dealt one after another.

The promise of warm pineapple upside-down cake, straight from the United Church Women's Cookbook of Swift Current, Saskatchewan. And the increasingly approving looks and engaging laugh of my attractive bridge partner.

Indeed, there had been times lately when I'd look at Janet and become almost dizzy with desire. I'd have to sit down for a bit and think about Sister Piranha until the spell passed.

It was possible this spell had less to do with Janet's siren appeal and more to do with Vunapope's rule of strict abstinence imposed on bachelor doctors such as myself.

In any case, unless I was entirely misreading her, Janet wasn't giving off strong sexual signals. She was friendly, certainly, and perhaps a touch flirtatious...?

I wasn't sure and it didn't matter. For me, her presence added a muted erotic glow to the evening.

As I laid down my cards and played the dummy to Janet's four hearts, something else made me glow inside…

Earlier in the day, Dawna had come to the outpatient clinic at the hospital.

At first I'd thought she was dropping by to confirm our date for bridge, but she held one of the yellow cards that Ruthie at Reception gave patients arriving for their medical appointments.

Dawna's face beamed as she entered my office. "Ross, I'm pregnant. Just about three months, but I'm not showing yet. Garnet is thrilled. And so am I."

My stomach plunged into ice water. What a disappointment that they would be leaving PNG so soon.

Although I'd given it little thought, I expected that Garnet and Dawna would complete their contract with Kokopo High School before starting a family.

They were only in their mid-twenties, so there was no hurry for them to have a child, and the school year was just getting started. Their premature departure would leave a huge hole in my life. I struggled to hide my disappointment.

With what I'd hoped was a casual, small-talk tone of voice, I raised a question: "Will you have the baby back in Swift Current near your family?"

"I'm going to deliver right here at Vunapope.," she grinned. "Don't look so surprised, Ross," Dawna chided playfully as my jaw dropped. "You and Sister Agatha have got a great reputation. Garnet and I know we'll be in good hands."

She pulled a pen and small notepad out of her bag. "Now, I'd like to know my exact due date."

"But Dawna," I protested, "lots of things can go wrong. We do our best here, but this isn't Canada, you know. What if there's a complication? Are you sure about this?"

"Heck," she scoffed, "my mother had six kids, even a set of twins, practically without batting an eyelash."

"I'm young, I'm healthy, and I've got good genes," she continued. "We've still got a year and a half left on our agreement with the high school, and we love PNG too much to even think about going home early."

"Well…" I said hesitantly, "let me check your blood pressure and do your urine test today. As long as you stay healthy, I'll be delighted to follow your pregnancy and deliver the baby. But I'm going to insist you go to Canada or Australia for the rest of your pregnancy if you develop diabetes – or if there are twins, or *triplets*, in there." I'd pointed towards her tummy and rolled my eyes in mock horror at the idea of triplets. "We'll set you up for a proper assessment next week in our prenatal clinic…"

My recollection was pleasantly interrupted by a sweet smell that summoned me back to the card game. Now, I was mentally as well as physically back in Dawna's front room.

As the room filled with the tantalizing aroma of Dawna's fresh baking, Janet was staring at her cards, apparently deciding which one to lead on the sixth trick.

Janet was well on her way to making our four hearts and the rubber, when an aged truck suddenly roared and coughed as it came to a stop on the driveway. A door creaked and banged.

My dummy hand was under Janet's control, so I stood up, walked over to the windows, and muttered, "I sure hope that's not Horace."

Standing beside the truck, a figure drew on a cigarette and scuffed at the dirt with his foot. I recognized the vehicle and the driver. "Dammit," I cursed, "it's Horace, all right. In the hospital's Land Cruiser. One of the sisters must have sent him."

I called out through the open louvers: "Horace. *You lookim me, Dokta?*"

"Yes, Dokta," Horace nodded. "Sister say you come to Maternity. Hurry-up-quick. *Wanpela meri i-got twins.*"

Horace climbed back into the truck and rumbled into the night. His mission was complete.

But my mission was just beginning.

I gripped the car keys resting at the bottom of my pocket, not wanting to take them out.

I longed to stay, to bask in delight as Janet finished off a spectacular game, to taste the syrupy sweetness of Dawna's upside-down cake, and to sip the chocolaty velvet of a mug of steaming Milo.

"Sorry Guys," I announced glumly. "Looks like I've gotta go back to the hospital right away. Some sort of trouble in the labour ward. A woman with twins."

Janet stood up and scanned the room for her purse. She forced a pout to her lips, but a smile shone through her eyes. "I hate to waste all these fantastic cards. We might've made – what d'you call it? – a slam?"

I nodded ruefully, realizing Janet had a role to play in what lay ahead. If the woman in the labour ward needed an emergency transfusion, Janet would have to do the testing, grouping, and matching. Of course, she would abandon the game and dash back with me to the hospital.

Garnet's apple-red face was overrun with happy dimples. "Aaw, too bad, Ross and Janet. You'll have to forfeit the second rubber. That makes a tie for the night. One rubber each."

Dawna had left the bridge table and was at the kitchen counter, wrapping something up on a couple of plates.

"Garnet! Really," Dawna playfully scolded her husband. "We'll concede this hand and the two rubbers. And thank you guys very much for a fun evening. You can each take some of the cake with you to have later on this evening."

She handed us each a plate and with a wink, gave her husband a look of feigned impatience. "Don't worry – there's plenty left for you, Garnet."

My Toyota's bald tires squealed as the car jolted to a halt at the hospital entrance.

Janet headed left towards the laboratory where she would tidy up her paperwork and wait by the phone for my call.

I headed right, pulled open the maternity wing's side door, and strode into the glare of the labour ward.

This was not the first time that I had the feeling I was bursting onto the stage of a one-act play; one already in progress with my part unscripted, unrehearsed, and demanding my moment-to-moment improvisation.

The other actors, anxiety in their faces, would press me to provide the cues crucial to driving the drama towards a gratifying conclusion. If a patient was hemorrhaging, choking, or suffocating, terror would strike me and ricochet as impatience and hostility.

I fought the stifling odour of too many bodies in the underventilated space.

The room, though designed for delivering babies, had the impersonal atmosphere of a bus station congested with anxious-looking passengers uncertain about their destinations.

Huddled against one wall were six nursing students wearing navy shits, white aprons, and lopsided caps.

Lined against the opposite wall, with no provision for privacy or modesty, were five iron-frame beds. Only one was occupied, but the woman on it filled the room with shrieks of desperation. She flapped a washcloth against her plump, earthy breasts and yelled, "Mama! Baby Jesus! Mama!"

The midwife, Sister Agatha, stood arms akimbo beside the woman's bed, her gaze fixed on the wall clock. She counted the drops from an intravenous bottle suspended from a pole and growled instructions at her team of anxious students.

Although fatigue and impatience were written in the lines above her jaw, I knew it was fear, not anger, that burned in Sister Agatha's eyes. She sensed danger like a she-wolf sniffing menace riding on the wind.

The top half of the patient glistened with sweat. Blood smeared her bottom half. An umbilical cord snaked out of her vagina and dangled over the end of her bed. A stainless steel clamp gripped the butt of the cord.

A smirk pressed against Sister Agatha's sharp, yellow teeth. "Sorry to take you away from your little card game, Dokta."

I set my shoulder blades and clenched my teeth while Sister yanked at the strings at the back of my gown and explained that the woman had arrived thirty minutes earlier and delivered immediately.

"And Dokta, no problems there were until after the baby was born. A second twin we discovered. It is still inside. And very high. Nowhere near the birth canal."

My knees felt numb and rubbery. It was now up to me to extract the second twin. I pictured Dawna's expanding belly and optimistic grin, and my throat tightened.

I smiled at the patient and palpated her abdomen. The second twin was jammed crosswise, high in the belly.

Now, I stared at my hands resting on the large tummy and considered my options.

Performing a Caesarean section would be fairly straightforward, but I had to decide against it. All over PNG, Caesareans were avoided as much as possible for fear that the uterus might rupture during a subsequent pregnancy and labour. If that happened in a village far from an operating theatre, mother and baby would die.

I would have to grope inside this woman's vagina, reach into her uterus, catch hold of one tiny foot, then the other, and pull the infant out feet-first. The manipulation would be painful, perhaps excruciating, and we had no equipment to give anaesthetics to labouring mothers.

Generations of celibate midwives in white habits had dictated that maternal anaesthesia for vaginal delivery was too dangerous for use at Vunapope. The nuns figured that obstetrical pain was expected, not harmful, and quickly forgotten.

A lack of anaesthesia was not apparent while my patient was resting on her bed in a state of quiet detachment after a generous injection of intravenous morphine.

Sister instructed one of the students to explain, in local dialect, what the dokta was about to do. I smiled again and made some noises that I hoped sounded reassuring.

I inserted my gloved hand into the woman's vagina. Her eyes filled with terror. When my fingers reached her uterus, she screamed and thrashed against her bloodied sheets and mattress. Sister turned to the students huddled against the far wall, snapped her fingers, and barked a set of orders.

Two stone-faced students shuffled over and grasped the woman's thighs. A third pulled the umbilical cord out of my way, keeping it safely clamped to prevent the bloodstream of the undelivered twin from hemorrhaging through it.

Sister injected a second dose of morphine. I waited a minute, closed my ears to the woman's shouts, and explored further into her uterus with my fingers. She bucked violently. The metal clamp ripped through the umbilical cord and clattered to the floor.

The cord recoiled, like a severed elastic, into the nether regions of the uterus. Its ruptured vessels, beyond all hope of retrieval and open to the bloodstream of the undelivered twin, gushed out of the vagina like a fire hose.

Rivers of sweat poured from my forehead. The baby's blood streamed into a crimson puddle at my feet. Panic threatened to seize me in its ice-cold grip.

A fetus cannot be pulled out by the hand. You have to grab a foot. Only a foot. I swallowed hard, closed my eyes, ignored everything in the world except the feeling in my fingertips, and groped again.

There it was, a little foot. Blood and amniotic fluid made it slippery. Very slippery. Its tiny toes wiggled as I grasped them between my thumb and forefinger.

The foot pulled away, a reflex from being tickled, and it was gone. I'd lost it! I opened my eyes and saw the expanding puddle of blood on the floor, now a manticore coming to life. I closed my eyes again, leaned into the screeching woman's pelvis, and slipped my hand farther into her uterus.

I touched a hand. No, it was a foot. Yes, a foot. My fingers had found a foot! I clenched its heel and ankle in a grip that mirrored my resolution.

Working quickly to accomplish the delivery before the baby bled to death, yet gently to avoid injuring mother and infant, I coaxed one foot, then the other, then the rump into the vagina.

With the baby in the breech position, I steeled myself for the manoeuvres that would liberate his shoulders, arms, and head. If I rushed this part of the delivery, the womb would tighten around his head and trap him in the birth canal. He would suffocate.

During an infinite two minutes, with my heart hammering at my throat, my arms trembling, and the baby spurting blood with every heartbeat, I eased his pint-size body past the perils and into the hush of the delivery room.

He felt warm, but he lay limp and lifeless in my hands. I blew at his face. He wrinkled his mouth and pushed a startled cry from his throat. He was still alive!

I clamped and cut his cord and rushed him over to a table. Sister motioned for one of the students to take my place, deliver the placenta, and complete the other routine tasks.

The little fellow was pale, like powdered talc, and as floppy as a cloth doll. He had lost so much blood that though his heart raced, his femoral pulse was imperceptible. He was in shock and would not last long.

How could I arrange to give him a blood transfusion quickly enough? We only had a few minutes before his heart would give out. Selecting an appropriate unit of blood from the blood bank by using even an abbreviated cross-match technique would take an hour, maybe longer. And there might not be a suitable unit among our inconsistent stock, sporadically allotted by the PNG Red Cross.

I remembered that Janet had once opened a drawer in the laboratory and shown me a list of the names and blood types of all the nurses, aides, and students at Vunapope Hospital. It had been Sister Agatha's idea to keep the list safe and up-to-date in a scribbler. They called it the "walking blood bank" because the blood was still inside its potential donors where it was waiting to be matched and withdrawn when needed. Being always fresh, it could never be past an expiry date.

Might it be possible for us to take blood from one of the nurses standing there at the bedside and inject it straight, without testing or matching, into the baby? It wouldn't take much to fill the empty

122

veins of a newborn, and the process would take only a few minutes from start to finish. The blood would be warm; it would contain no harmful preservatives; its most fragile constituents would be intact. The Rh factor would be irrelevant because every Papua New Guinean was genetically Rh positive. We would just need type O, the Universal Donor.

Such a direct transfusion was an unorthodox notion, unthinkable in Canada. I studied Sister Agatha's face. Lines of strain creased her cheeks and crept beneath her veil. I gazed at the clock, then at the baby, hovering on the verge of life. I looked back at the clock. I whispered my idea into Sister's ear. She nodded and slipped out to ring the laboratory. With luck, Janet would still be puttering there.

I explained my plan to the flock of nurses gaping at the infant. When Janet burst breathlessly through the door with her scribbler in her hand, she was greeted by a crush of girls calling out their names. They all wanted to be the donor.

Four of the students were type O. I looked at Sister Agatha and shrugged. Who should it be?

Sister pointed to a stocky student with thick calves and huge hands. She was standing apart from the others; her course features were bloated with tears, her red eyes filled with shame.

When she pulled down her mask, I realized the girl was Adelina, the take-charge student who had shown so much skill during the methanol crisis. She had been pulling on the cord when it had snapped.

The growl had gone from Sister's voice. "Adelina – would you like to donate your blood to the baby?"

Adelina bit on her lower lip and nodded.

Janet led Adelina over to one of the unoccupied delivery beds and asked her to lie down. The other girls giggled. They weren't yet ready to imagine themselves in labour.

Janet pulled a glass slide, a tiny blade, and a couple of small bottles from the pocket of her dress. "Ross, let me do a quick check to be sure Adelina really is type O. It won't take a minute."

"Okay. I'll get the baby ready for the transfusion. Sister, I'll need you to bring me a few things."

To infuse the blood into the baby, I placed a tiny tube into his umbilical vein, the wide vessel leading from his belly button toward his heart.

I used his weight and ghostly appearance to estimate how much blood he had lost, and figured I'd start with three or four syringes and observe his response.

Meanwhile, Janet got ready to withdraw aliquots of Adelina's blood by inserting a needle into a vein near the young woman's elbow.

As soon as I gave a nod, Janet filled the first syringe and placed it into an enamel basin, which someone had lined with a crisply pressed tea towel.

A student, eyes bulging and tongue clenched between her lips, carried the basin across the room and handed it to me. I lifted the syringe, connected it to the tube in the baby's navel, and injected the warm, dark, liquid.

Nothing happened. The baby stayed motionless, quiet, and ashen. Each breath was shallow and rapid, like a sparrow's.

The student returned with a second syringe filled with Adelina's type O. Still, there was no change.

As I injected the third syringe, a flush of pink leapt into the infant's face. He let out a peep. The nurses, gathered around us in a semicircle, let out a gasp.

With the fourth syringe, the baby opened his eyes, raised his arms, and tightened his fists.

The room, which had been as quiet as a mausoleum, erupted in happy girlish chatter that sounded like birdsong.

I removed the tube from the infant's navel, tied a suture through the vessels to make sure they wouldn't bleed, and wrapped the baby to keep him warm.

Then, I handed him to Adelina. She cradled him in her muscular arms, stared into his pink face, and was struck again by a torrent of tears.

As I pulled off my gloves, Janet gave my arm a soft squeeze. I wondered how well the sweat on my cheeks masked the puddles spilling from my eyes.

10

Fine Lines

Freddy's corner of the children's ward looked like Noah's ark. Over the preceding weeks, the ten year-old had created dozens of birds, animals, and insects out of sheets of newspaper.

Using only scissors and a wooden ruler, he had snipped and folded the pages of the *Papua New Guinea Post-Courier* into a dominion of creatures, real and imagined.

Long-tailed butterflies floated from the rafters, birds of paradise preened on the windowsill, and baby crocodiles romped across the floor.

My favourite was a rhinoceros beetle, ten times normal size, which stood guard on the foot of Freddy's bed.

And where Freddy was headed, he was going to need the very best of guardians.

As I approached him, taking care not to trample a pair of swans swimming among the crocodiles, I listened to the gentle snores of the small artist I'd come to love.

The air was heavy with the smell of decay, like weeds rotting in a ditch on a steamy summer day.

His body was a battlefield of purple bruises and oozing needle tracks, of swollen lips and bleeding gums.

A flask of intravenous morphine, hanging on a pole above Freddy's head, signalled that a truce had been declared.

We had conceded our fight against his aggressive leukemia and were now at peace.

In the face of the inevitable events playing out in Freddy's body, I had been forced to change my role from eager physician-scientist, my pockets stuffed with curatives, to modest doctor-healer, who knows no higher calling than the relief of suffering.

I'd first encountered Freddy about six months earlier. He was sitting at a table in the children's ward, drawing intricate lines on a sheet of newspaper.

If you'd told me that he was visiting from another solar system, I would have believed you. Hanging limply like the strands of silk on a cob of corn, his hair was straight and white, an oddity in this part of the world. His skin, the colour of brown clay, was dotted with light and dark spots.

At first, I thought he'd been spattered with two colours of paint, walnut and ivory, but the pattern was natural. He'd been born that way.

He had stubby thumbs, and his fingers, fused by webs of skin, formed lobster claws that handled the pencil and ruler with speedy dexterity.

Though Freddy was only the height of a four year-old, the sentences that arose from his quirky voice box startled me with their high-pitched squeakiness and their confident intelligence.

"*Wanum name belong you?*" I asked, glancing at his chart.

"Freddy Tovina." The boy's lips were as pale as coconut meat. "You're the doctor?" He looked intently at my arms, eyeing the freckles that covered them.

"Yes, that's right. It says here you have a bad cough."

Freddy coughed out a rat-a-tat, wiped the snot from his nose with the back of a pincer-like hand, and then picked up a pair of scissors.

He studied the pattern he'd drawn across the columns of the *Post-Courier*. "Have you seen a stonefish, Dokta? They've got lots of spots, and they sting if you step on them. This one won't sting. You can have it when it's done."

I smiled in response. "I'd like to listen to your breathing."

Freddy pulled off his tee shirt and continued cutting and folding while I caught the sounds of his pneumonia echoing through my stethoscope.

My hands felt the sweaty fever that shivered through his small frame.

"We're going to take a little blood test, Freddy, and give you some medicine."

He made a face and coughed again, louder and longer than before. "I don't like needles," he protested. "Not even little ones."

The test confirmed that his white lips were caused by anaemia: his red blood cells had dipped to half the normal level.

I imagined that the PNG triad of malaria, intestinal parasites, and a diet poor in iron had depleted his red cells.

I treated him with antibiotics for his pneumonia, chloroquine for malaria, medicine for the worms in his belly, and then iron and a blood transfusion for his anaemia.

Within a few days he was scampering around the ward, lips pink, cured of his cough and fever. The nurses sent him home, and I put his stonefish on top of my fridge.

A month later, Freddy was back. The pink had faded from his lips, and he was listless and breathless. He lay propped on a pillow, his scissors and newspapers ignored inside a string bag on the floor beneath his bed.

I repeated his blood tests. They confirmed that the anaemia had returned; his red cells were lower than ever.

This time, his stock of platelets – the tiny blocks the body stacks to build blood clots – had become depleted.

I examined him carefully, this time taking a closer look at the odd shape of his arms and hands. I sent him next door to Sister Gertrude for X-rays of his upper limbs.

Sister Gertrude was elderly, impatient, and stingy with her X-ray film; she didn't want it wasted on unnecessary tests, and often returned patients to the ward with fewer X-ray views than I would have liked.

I imagined the crotchety sigh Sister Gertrude would heave when Freddy appeared at her door with my request that she X-ray both his arms from the elbows to the fingertips. But this time she came running into the children's ward as fast as her arthritic hips and knees would waddle.

"Dokta. Look at these pictures." She always called them pictures. Perhaps she considered herself an artist. "That boy is missing the radius bone from each forearm. And see," she said, stabbing the film with an knobby finger, "a bone from each thumb missing also. I am never seeing anything like it."

My breath caught in my throat. I was out of my depth.

The bookshelf in my office held a photographic atlas of children with distorted features and assorted deformities. Freddy was so distinctive that I figured I just might spot his double if I pulled out the textbook and flipped through its pictures. There he was on page two hundred thirty-four. Under a headline that declared "Fanconi Anaemia," a familiar face stared at me with a shy grin and spattered cheeks. Silky hair floated over his ears.

The blurb below the photograph described Freddy almost perfectly: short stature, spotted skin, webbed fingers, bones missing from the thumbs and forearms, and eyelids that looked too small for the elfin face. The condition was hereditary, created when two parents each passed to an offspring their hidden Fanconi gene. By acting together, the child's two copies of the gene came out of hiding to produce the disorder.

Freddy had learned to live with his defective parts, which the textbook politely called anomalies.

It was the future maelstrom in his bone marrow that caused my stomach to jump into my chest. The book predicted that Freddy was headed for disaster.

He was alone in a rowboat, upstream of an enormous waterfall;

but only I could see the spray and hear the roar of the murderous cataract that lay in his path. No lifeline could divert him from his fate, so it was pointless to startle him with whistles and tip him overboard while he floated on calm waters.

Once again, the nurses and I patched Freddy up and sent him home to his village. Thereafter, he returned to Vunapope with his mother and his siblings every few weeks for checkups and blood transfusions.

With his bone marrow only limping along, Freddy needed regular infusions of red blood cells to keep his lips pink and a spring in his step.

Once a month, the family trundled up the hill to the hospital from the bus stop on the coastal road. Freddy's mother always had a toddler by the hand, an infant on her hip, and a smile on her face. Across her back she lugged her enormous string bag, a *bilum*, crocheted at home in the traditional style from colourful nylon yarn.

She stuffed the *bilum* with a pillow and blankets for the baby, betel nuts for herself, and the thermos flask, aluminum dishes, and packets of food from which she prepared their meals during the daylong sessions at the hospital. She never asked questions, but seemed to sense that we were doing our best for her son who was so different from everyone else in her village.

One day, after half-a-year of carefree checkups and transfusions, I noticed that Freddy's smile was missing.

His spotted skin had tiny purple bleeding points, and his lips were raw. Painful sores had sprung like weeds inside his mouth and down his throat.

I knew what we were on the lookout for, and Janet found it in her laboratory within minutes of taking a few drops of blood from the tip of Freddy's finger.

Janet was breathless on her end of the telephone. "Ross... Freddy's white count. It's a hundred and ten thousand. At first, I thought I'd erred. You know, with the decimal point. But there's no mistake. That's the highest white count I've ever seen."

"I was afraid that's what you'd find."

"You were expecting leukemia, huh? On the smear, they look like myeloblasts."

"Yeah, AML." Freddy had slipped from anaemia into acute myeloblastic leukemia. "Kids with Fanconi's often get it."

"Geez," Janet said, her voice shaking. "Poor little guy. Is there much you can do for him, Ross?"

That was the question. How much *could* I do for him? AML, a cancer of the white blood cells, was usually fatal, even in medical centres at the best universities.

Our only hope lay in an expensive and complex schedule of cancer-fighting medications, at least four of them.

Freddy would also need state-of-the-art blood products and exotic antibiotics.

We had none, and transporting Freddy from his Iron Age village to a more sophisticated country was no more a possibility than sending him to Jupiter.

"I'm not sure what I can do, Janet. I'll have to ask Sister Leora. Maybe she can call one of her pharmacy contacts in Port Moresby."

The idea of fighting Freddy's cancer with exotic drugs buoyed me with excitement.

I would have the latest treatment flown in just for him; I'd save his life, right here under the palm trees. But another part of me was so afraid that Sister Leora's call would be successful that I nearly told her not to bother. The child's plight brought back a haunting memory…

Still fresh in my mind were the events of one night in a children's cancer ward in Canada.

I had been making my rounds as the junior intern on duty when the alarm on a cardiac monitor echoed down the corridor.

The siren blared out from Emily's room, where cancer was gnawing at the pre-schooler's brain, after months of radiation and chemotherapy had proven powerless against the advances of her tumour.

Emily's heart had finally given up. Her fight was over. Death had delivered her from agony and misery.

But four of us sprinted into her room, and I found myself pounding on her chest, bruising her ribs with frantic blows of CPR.

My superior spurred me with orders he hollered through clenched teeth.

When I should have been straightening Emily's bedclothes and consoling her parents, I instead followed orders to jolt her with adrenaline and electricity. I clutched the defibrillator panels in my sweaty palms and dealt a final thrust.

The monitor sprang to life. Bright signals flicked and danced in lively rhythms across its screen. I'd jump-started her heart like the rusty engine of a jalopy. Then I ran to the toilet and filled it with vomit.

Each time I walked past her door over the next few weeks, anger overwhelmed me. I didn't know where to aim it. At myself, for inflicting further torture on a dying four year-old, or at my supervisor for commanding me to keep her alive?

Emily existed on a futile regimen of excruciating needles and mutilating medicines.

She couldn't see or swallow; she couldn't wiggle her toes or point her fingers; but she could feel every jab, and she moaned like an injured kitten abandoned at the roadside.

Sister Leora did make the call to Port Moresby's pharmacy, and she let loose her sweetest Georgia charm on an unsuspecting bureaucrat in the capital city.

He agreed to airfreight a chemotherapy starter kit from the government's central pharmacy.

I got caught up in the spirit of the medical adventure and pestered the clerk in our mailroom every day, insisting there *must* be a parcel from Port Moresby.

Each time, I came away with empty hands and shattered hopes. When the packet finally arrived, I tore through its wrapper and pried open the mailer box; but after discarding the crinkled wads of newsprint inside, I was only left with two small vials. In the face of Freddy's terrifying cancer cells, they looked pathetically inadequate.

I followed the directions inside the package, dripped the drugs into Freddy's veins, and watched eagerly for signs that the medicines were working.

Freddy's mouth sores melted, and he ate a little of the sweet potato his mother patiently cooked and mashed in coconut cream.

His white count came down to normal.

He looked almost lively. He sat outside under the mango trees, pulled paper and tools out of his *bilum*, and set to work.

Every child in the ward soon had one of Freddy's creatures on their bed.

But the effects of the medicines lasted only two weeks. The cancerous white cells tripled in number.

Freddy's mouth erupted with ragged sores; the aches in his legs brought tears to his spotted cheeks; he huddled under his bed sheets.

Sister Leora pleaded with Port Moresby, but they'd depleted their stock of chemotherapy medicines. They'd nothing to send us.

I slipped past Freddy's paper menagerie and sat down on his mattress. I had to fight against the rotten smell of his breath gagging my throat.

His warm, bruised hand felt soft and smooth in mine, like a fine leather glove. As I listened to the rhythm of his snoring, I remembered the day we had first discovered his leukemia.

Janet had asked if there was much I could do for him.

Sitting now on Freddy's bed beside his family, holding his rhinoceros beetle and watching the morphine drip quietly into his veins, I felt awash in conflicting waves of sadness and serenity.

The remoteness of our island setting cradled us within a sanctuary far from the excesses of modern medicine.

Here, there was nothing more I could do *to* Freddy, but much I would do *for* him; I would stifle his discomfort, honour his dignity, and let him drift away in a state of peace.

11
Shells

For a tin-roofed doctor's office near the equator, my consulting room felt surprisingly comfortable.

The room's ancient ceiling fan stirred the air just enough to simulate coolness on the skin, the monotonous racket of the whirring blades spinning a cocoon of privacy.

Such seclusion was a rarity at Vunapope, where life in congested convents and regimented dormitories created insatiable appetites for gossip and tales of scandal.

It seemed that every nun and priest, being mindful of the sins of Cain, was an expert brother's keeper.

I opened the door and welcomed the next patient in from the fiery midday sunshine. The woman's *meri-blouse* flashed fiesta pink peonies on bright blue polyester, but the puffy eyelids on her mahogany face hinted at an infinite sadness. A hairless patch on the top of her scalp was, upon closer inspection, a callus formed by the lifetime of heavy loads she had carried on her head.

Unwrapping the tattered bandages from her arm, I caught a whiff of fermented sweat.

I removed the plaster splint and inspected my handiwork. The lacerated skin had healed beautifully, and without infection. There'd just be an ugly scar. I plucked out the dozen sutures I'd inserted some weeks earlier when she had arrived with a bloodied rag around her forearm, hiding the gash that zigzagged between her wrist and elbow. The wound, a gaping snarl of flesh and sinew, had threatened to cripple her hand. I'd managed to reconnect all her severed tendons, and now delighted at the flickers of movement in her thumb and fingers.

But even today, the woman remained mute. With shame? Guilt? Anger?

Her sister had explained that the husband had attacked her with a broken beer bottle. I'd seen such injuries many times before, and though I could repair the flesh, I could barely comprehend the deeper misery that alcohol inflicted. As the outsider doctor, I was kept blind to the dynamics of village life, where men seemed to rule as raucous kings and women served as docile beasts of burden.

I returned my patient to the bright sun. She shuffled off with a thank you on her lips and resignation in her eyes. On the outside, New Britain shined like a jewelled postcard of turquoise bays, emerald peaks, opal clouds, and sapphire skies. But the dim light filtering into the depths of village life reflected a grim picture where gems had little chance to sparkle.

Janet Lundquist slipped into my office through the open door and beamed her broad smile.

"What's up, Janet? Have they sent that bulb from Port Moresby, yet?" We couldn't be expected to run this place without a microscope.

"Yeah," Janet grinned, "it arrived yesterday. It's even the right size." Her voice always bubbled with vigour. Her eyes, though bloodshot, were sparkling. "I've been peering into the scope all morning, catching up on a backlog of tests."

She wiped the sweat from her face with her fingertips, then reached into the pocket of her white cotton shift. "Look at these shells, Ross. Aren't they beauties?"

Her hand held three seashells, each pristine with unblemished

134

markings. "I found these out on the reef," she added. "In the shallow water, not far from Vunapope Wharf. The most perfect tiger cowries I've ever seen. And look at this fabulous cone shell. It looks so innocent. You'd never know its stinger was poisonous."

I picked up a cowrie, fingered its smoothness, and carefully sniffed it. No nasty smell of fish or putrefaction. No hint of the tenacious creature that had once lived inside. "How did you clean them out?"

"Lucia from the high school showed me. You bury the live shells in the garden for two or three weeks. The little animal inside dies and rots in the soil." She made a face. "Yeah, I know. It sounds cruel. Anyway, the ants carry off the disgusting stuff that seeps out. These ones were a bit stinky when I dug them up, but I rinsed them in cold water for few minutes, and look at them. Fantastic specimens for my collection."

I handed back the glinting cowrie, its graceful dome beautifully speckled in browns and black. "I haven't had much luck digging the fleshy stuff out of my shells," I said. "It stays stuck deep inside and stinks up the house. Rosa throws them away. She can't stand the smell when she comes to do my laundry."

Janet smiled, then wrapped her nearly perfect specimens in tissue and slid them back into her pocket. "May I sit down, Ross? I didn't just come to show you my shells." A nervous crack went through her voice. She glanced furtively out the window. "I've come as a patient."

"Sure," I replied. "Have a seat. Tell me, what's wrong?"

"Oh, nothing's wrong. I feel fine." She rubbed her hands together and stared at them as if they contained a secret. "I was just wondering. Would you put me on the pill? You know, so I won't get pregnant?"

I sat stunned and immobilized. My mouth went dry. My heart galloped into my throat. In this original and exciting way, she was letting me know she was ready to take our relationship to a higher level. But she'd caught me off guard. All along, I must have been misreading her cues. We'd flirted lightly, shared beers around a table of friends at the golf club, played bridge and talked of home, seashells and photography during outings at the beach. But she'd always kept her distance. I'd felt friendship, but no waves of tenderness. No overture to a kiss. And now, this direct invitation, which startled me with its candour.

I'd adapted well to my position as the chaste and celibate doctor at Vunapope. In fact, I figured I was thriving as the high priest of orthopedics, therapeutics, and obstetrics. I was sharing intimate moments of people's lives, guiding them through times of crisis, and then retreating to a comfortable separateness within a shell so natural that I barely noticed it. My carapace provided both a doorway out and a hiding place within. Like a tortoise, I carried my shell with me and decided when and how far to venture beyond.

Janet, I surmised, was now offering something new. A sharing of the shell. A cure for loneliness. An exciting sexual partnership. But there were risks and complications; Father Barrow had made that clear. He had spoken plainly in the car after meeting me at the airport the first day I landed at Rabaul. If I had an *affair* with any of the women living at the mission, I would be shipped home, instantly, to Canada. No appeal.

The tone of Father's Irish brogue made his meaning unmistakable. "I sent our last bachelor doctor home to Australia on the very day I discovered a nursing student had been spending cozy nights in his house. They'll be no second chances, Doctor."

What a conflict. I'd dreamt for years about working in the South Seas, and now the dream was real. I loved the patients, the dramatic moments, the hard-won respect of the crusty nuns and priests. I could never endure the disgrace that an affair might lead to. But Janet had broached her proposal in a way that sounded difficult to refuse.

I retreated to the safety of my familiar role where I knew The Doctor's lines by heart. "Well, let me check your blood pressure – to be sure it's safe for you to take the pill." I reached for my stethoscope, reassured by the smoothness of its Bakelite bell and the familiar smell of its natural rubber tubing.

My mouth felt so dry that I could barely get my tongue to form the words. "Have... have you been on the pill before?"

Her cheeks flushed, and the base of her neck blossomed into a bed of pink blotches. "No. I haven't had a serious boyfriend before."

The stethoscope slipped from my sweaty hands and clattered to the floor. She wanted *me* as her first serious boyfriend? The directness of her approach was delightful, but the potential consequences of a relationship invited disaster. Would we be able to pull it off? Could we stay at the mission as dutiful coworkers by day and impassioned lovers by night? There was something deliciously exciting about staying one step ahead of the ill-humoured matron, Sister Pirmina.

I fumbled with the blood pressure cuff and got a proper reading on my second try: 120 over 80. Perfect.

"Well, sure, Janet," I said in what I hoped was a calm voice. "I can put you on the pill. Your blood pressure is fine."

"That's fantastic!" She beamed. "Kent will be pleased. We've been using condoms for the past couple of weeks, but we don't really like them."

Kent? She was sleeping with Kent Eastman! The muscular mechanic from Australia. Kent, the guy with the talent to fix almost anything. He'd retrieved the methylated spirits and lit the hurricane lamps that night the power failed at the golf club. Had he lit Janet's heart at the same time?

I pictured condoms strewn among the dust bunnies and Wilbur Smith paperbacks beneath his bed. His tiny bungalow faced the soccer pitch, directly across from the priests' residence; had Janet been sneaking in and out of there while the priests observed her movements from the wicker chairs on their veranda?

Blood flooded my cheeks and lit my ears. The tenderness in her smile and the blush of vulnerability on her neck were meant for him, not for me. Mortified that my dancing eyes and eager lips had betrayed my misconception, I set my jaw. Could she see the loneliness behind the colour in my face? Could she sense my desolation? No, she was thinking only of him. Of hearty Kent, who delivered bliss and carnal pleasure, while I dealt prudent counsel and provided pills. The bitter taste of my breakfast coffee seeped up from my stomach and stung the back of my throat.

And then my mind could see the white-haired priests lined up on their veranda, binoculars in hand, ogling Janet. I could almost hear their indignant chatter, like a parliament of budgies flitting and squawking at a passing cat. When I thought of the scandal and disgrace that I'd escaped, an incoming tide of relief drifted slowly over my heartache, and began to wash away some of the bitterness.

I managed to unset my jaw, look into Janet's face, and ask a final few professional questions. I then picked up a notepad, wrote out the prescription, and signed my name to it with an exaggerated flourish. Although I felt the lingering pangs of disappointment, my palms were dry, and my heart – having retreated from my throat – beat quietly again inside my chest.

Suddenly my moment of acute embarrassment ended. Through the window I heard a rumble of frantic footsteps, the slamming of doors, the distant sounds of screams and sobs. A dog's staccato barking punctured the air.

Janet stuffed her prescription into the pocket of her dress and peered out between the louvers. "There's a herd of flip-flops running towards the E.R. And that dog sounds real frightened. But I can't see what's going on."

I tore open the door and we stepped into the blazing sunlight, looking left towards the jumbled sounds of fear and panic. We joined the rush of bodies, dressed in white and blue, scrambling towards an untended grassy thicket across the driveway from the hospital.

Before I could see it, I knew something horrible lay in the tall brush. The rushing, barking, crying, all spoke of terror.

As the anxious throng swept me through the shoulder-high grass, sharp blades of vegetation whipped at my knees and lashed at my face. A suffocating pungency of rotting flesh enveloped my nose and lips. Then came the frenzied sound of buzzing flies.

Perhaps they'd found Amigo, the friendly mutt who roamed the mission, living off scraps of rice and fish tossed from the back door of the nursing students' residence. Had our mongrel mascot finally lost a canine broil?

No, the body, splayed out on a boggy path and half-covered in hastily uprooted shoots of *kunai* grass, was not Amigo's. The uniform was unmistakable. Sickeningly so. The dark blue shift was smudged with mud and torn at the neck and hemline. The once bright face, now bloodied and bloated, betrayed the blows and fury of a vicious attack. But worst of all, a swarm of flies sucked greedily at the mucus dribbling from the corners of still-open eyes.

"Mother of God," I exclaimed. "Who is it?"

"It's Adelina, Dokta."

"Are you sure?"

Veronika nodded. "She's been missing for three days. See the tattoos above her nose?" she said, sweeping her fingers across the chevrons on her own glistening forehead. "I know them well. I did them for her." The young nurse's confident face crinkled into sobs and tears, her familiar regal presence collapsing.

A deep, female voice boomed in Teutonic tones from the roadway behind us. "What's going on here? Agnes and Helwig, you're supposed to be on duty. What silliness are you gawking at? You'll never learn anything by such gawking."

It was Sister Agatha from Maternity Ward bounding towards us. "Dokta, I see you've come to sniff and gawk along with all my staff. Shouldn't you be..."

I didn't have to point. What lay before us was all too clear. "It's Adelina, Sister."

"Lord have mercy. Oh no!" She covered her face with her massive hands and heaved a giant's sobs into her palms. "Oh no. *Bitte!* Please, it can't be. Not again. *Halte sie auf, Mama!*" She pulled a blue hanky from her pocket. "*Bitte, Mama.* Make them stop. *Bitte!*" Covering her nose and mouth with the large, striped hanky, she turned and ran towards the hospital leaving a choppy wake of tears and wails.

Janet put her arm around Veronika's crumpling frame and held her upright. The young woman buried her face in the shoulder of the tall American and moaned. Janet stared at me and opened her mouth, but no words found their way out. Her eyes, huge and green, said it clearly: "What do we do now?"

A bludgeoned corpse lay at my feet, Sister Agatha had bolted in an unexpected breakdown of nerve, a dozen of my students stood weeping and keening in a semicircle beside me, and nausea gripped my belly in a stranglehold while the stench of rotting flesh invaded my pores and stuffed my nostrils. I just stood there and stared at the swarming, menacing flies.

"Should I... call the police... Dokta?" The hesitant utterance in a startling baritone came from Joseph, the evening orderly from the men's ward. My Angel Gabriel, who mumbled sage advice when it was needed most, had been partially hidden by the clutch of sobbing nurses.

"Joseph! One of our students. Murdered."

"Yes, Dokta." Again, those rounded shoulders and doleful eyes, seeming to accept the blame. He slowly shook his head and clucked his tongue. I waited, hoping he'd unravel the story, tell me when and how and why this had happened. But he just looked at me expectantly, bright red betel juices trickling from the corners of his mouth.

I nodded slowly. "Yes. Call the police, Joseph. *Tenkyu*. And tell them to come *hurry-up-kwik*."

Joseph stepped up on his toes and swept his arms in big circles that pointed towards the hospital buildings behind us. The force and confidence in his voice surprised me. "*Yupela i-go. Dispela meri i-die pinis, na yupela i-mas go back long work belong yupela.*"

Like a shepherd, he corralled the distraught and skittish students and had them trudging through the field, away from the scene and back to the driveway. And maybe back to their work. I watched as he positioned two burly nursing students, Mathius and Julius, to keep the curious from encroaching beyond the roadway.

Janet, Veronika, and I stood guard on the grassy path, as if keeping company with Adelina's broken and partly hidden body. The stench forced us to maintain our vigil from some distance, but we stayed close enough, it seemed, so that she would know we were there. An unspoken understanding passed among the three of us. The relentless rays of the unclouded sun stung my eyes and scorched my forehead. Half an hour stretched into a lifetime before the contingent of three uniformed constables arrived from Kokopo's police station. They looked as awkward as boys at a high-school dance:

having made their appearance, they didn't quite know how to make the first move.

Sister Pirmina arrived at the same time. She strutted past us to see the body for herself, the police officers following like obedient goslings. She returned alone with a face of stone. When she thinned her lips across her tiny pointed teeth, and motioned me towards her for a private word, I braced myself for one of her harangues.

"I told the police to take Adelina's body to the morgue at Nonga hospital." She shook her head slightly and took a deep breath. "I've just come from our convent. Sister Agatha is in no state to continue with her duties in Maternity." She looked deep into my eyes as if determining that I'd witnessed Sister's outburst. "Her emotions have run away with her," Sister Pirmina added. "Luckily, Sister Bettina from our mission in New Ireland is visiting. I've assigned her to be in charge of Maternity for these times being. Sister Bettina is an experienced midwife, but too softhearted to run the ward with efficiency for long. She'll do for now."

"What do you think happened to Adelina, Sister? Was it a stranger, or..."

"Really, Dokta," she said dismissively. "A stranger didn't murder Adelina. She was engaged to a brute from her village. A cocoa labourer who had before beaten her. I was arranging to next week send her on a posting. Far away. To Uvol Island. He must have found out. I blame her parents for trying to force a ridiculous union. The man can barely tell time, let alone read and write."

She fiddled with her veil and scratched at her glistening hairline. "But the police will never prove anything. They may look very fine in their matching shirts and shorts, and shiny black boots, but about detective work they know almost nothing. And Adelina – one of our best students. Sister Agatha had recommended her for the midwifery course. To start next year in Port Moresby. What a foolish girl, she should never have gone off alone with that man."

I clenched my fists inside my pockets. Sister possessed an unlimited capacity for flinging hurtful barbs; she even had jabs for the freshly deceased.

Reluctantly, we tramped out of the field, leaving the body of Adelina with the constables.

A swarm of onlookers buzzed on the tarmac in front of the hospital. Grizzled patients had limped up from the men's ward on homemade canes and crutches. Tear-streaked nurses consoled one another with murmurs and hugs. Wide-eyed mothers suckled squirming babies, while snotty-nosed children jockeyed within the milling density of the throng. Everyone was hoping for a good look at the body as it emerged from the tall grass.

The stretcher appeared, teetering between the arms of the diffident policemen; its flimsy shroud fluttered in the steamy noontime breezes. When two dogs charged, growling and snapping at the corpse's naked feet, anguished hoots and gasps erupted from the crowd.

The cumbrous stretcher bucked and scraped along the floor of the police van; the rear door shut with a brutal slam. The brusqueness stirred a stewpot of emotions. Anger broke the surface. I wanted to shout at the cops: show Adelina more respect; do you have to be so careless and so insolent?

The vehicle roared off towards Rabaul, leaving a haze of blue smoke and a mission family in fear and fascination of the lethal scandal unfolding in our midst.

Over the following days, melancholia covered the mission.

We did our work but seldom looked each other in the eye, as if to do so would weave consolidated images from the fragile threads that drifted through the private places in our minds.

We could cope with unrealized thoughts, but we knew that any crystallized notion of what had happened would strike with the force of concrete bricks.

The only social unit not disturbed by the tragedy was the ginger-feathered hen that slept with her brood in a hideout abutting my kitchen wall. Louise was a conscientious mother who produced chicks in sequential batches from her nest, an earthen hollow wedged between the cinderblock foundation and my propane tank. She pecked the ground for seeds and insects and clucked with enthusiasm upon discovery of every delicious tidbit; whenever cheeky chicks waddled out of line, she squawked in reprimand.

Every day after breakfast she set off for adventures beyond the garden, a dozen cheepers behind her; each afternoon she returned to the yard to settle her gang of fluffy rovers into the hideaway and under her wings. Sometimes there was a chick or two fewer than had set off in the morning, the vanished-ones having fallen victim to the likes of dogs, cats, and pythons.

As soon as yellow chicks matured into independent, russet adolescents, the reassuring cycle of eggs, hatchlings, and saucy youngsters started anew. The consistency of Louise's parenting patterns, and her unfailing loyalty to our relationship, comforted me. No matter what disappointments I faced at the hospital, the plump ginger hen and her family were happily nestled near my kitchen door by day's end, and calling out for breadcrumbs and bits of papaya at breakfast next morning.

A few days after Adelina's tear-filled funeral, a stifling afternoon found me once again at the business end of a delivery table. When the birth of an infant surged into a nightmare of unexpected complications, my heart raced and my stomach roiled.

Instead of calling me at the first hint that a delivery was in trouble, the nurses too often delayed their summons until the baby's suffocation was nearly complete, the mother's bloodstream was glistening from a puddle on the floor, and panic was tattooed on the face of every person in the room.

Sister Bettina – still pinch-hitting in Maternity for the distressed and indisposed Sister Agatha – looked like a flustered, kindly aunt. Her veil and wimple were tilted askew, and streaks of blood slashed across her sterile gown.

She held her small, gloved hands interlocked in front of her chest. Was it prayer or anxiety that made her hold them so? Concern, not hostility, pinched her face. She looked like a mother worried for the safety of a child.

Breathless, she thanked me for coming so quickly. "It is a

breech birth. The body I delivered, but the head, it will not come out. In the cervix, it is stuck."

We had to work fast. The infant could suffocate in a matter of moments.

"Give the woman two full ampoules of pethidine and another of Valium," I instructed. "Straight into her vein. As fast as you can." Our only hope was that the drugs would quell the spasm that had turned the cervix into a muscular vice. "And bring a syringe of Narcan." If either the mother or infant stopped breathing after such a large dose of pethidine, I could reverse the effect with Narcan.

I had never seen anyone work so quickly. Sister Bettina had the drugs drawn up and injected into the woman's arm as fast I donned a gown and gloves. The woman closed her eyes and started snoring. I eased the baby out through the relaxed cervix. Three puffs of oxygen and the baby was screaming angrily. We woke the mother with Narcan but the Valium kept her in a muted haze.

When my work was done, I shuffled out of the delivery room and dropped into one of a pair of wooden armchairs in the courtyard. The maternity ward's central square buzzed like a marketplace with the chortles of women kibitzing with their girlfriends, the impatient howls of hungry babies, and the low-pitched moans of labouring mothers who paced and lumbered in progressive stages of distress. I was thankful to be left collecting myself in the shade of a ficus tree.

Sister Bettina approached with a huge smile and a large tea tray. She had repositioned her veil, donned a crisply pressed apron, and washed the spatters of blood from her spectacles. Like Beatrix Potter's diminutive Mrs. Tiggy-winkle – the motherly hedgehog in white bonnet and housedress – she was everyone's friend who could put everything right. The china cups rattled on their saucers in time with Sister's footsteps, and steam rose from the mouth of the kettle.

I beamed when I spotted a familiar flash of red tartan, an oblong packet containing Scottish shortbread. It was impossible to imagine how those biscuits could journey all the way to the shores of New Britain from a modest bakery seven miles from my father's childhood home.

"Already, the baby is on the breast." She set the heavy tray on the table beside me, taking care not to spill the boiling water. "Now, for *our* refreshment it is the time. They tell me you like cookies, yah?" There was music in her German accent. The light notes of Mozart.

I ripped open the packet of shortbread without waiting for any further invitation.

"That was a close call, Sister. Too close"

"Yes. Next time, I am sooner calling you."

The first few gulps of tea slid down my thirsty throat so quickly that I barely noticed them. I was on my second cup, and my third cookie, when I asked how Sister Agatha was doing.

"She is all day spending in her room, only coming out for morning Mass, and sometimes for a meal."

I dunked shortbread into my tea. The Scottish biscuits had toughened into disappointing hardtack during their protracted ocean voyage. "She really took Adelina's death hard. I didn't think anything could shock Sister Agatha. She always seems so strong." We exchanged knowing looks that gave permission for the other to speak candidly. "And so stern," I added.

Sister nodded. "I am thinking it was the sight of the battered body."

"She's seen worse things, surely."

"Yes. In Germany, at the end of the war."

"But she would've been a child at that time. Too young to nurse the wounded."

"But not too young to witness her village by Russian soldiers attacked and burned – after officially the war was over."

"Russian soldiers?"

Sister Bettina then told me the story of Silesia, a German province I'd never heard of: At the end of World War II, when the Allies divided up the geographical and political spoils, Silesia was handed over to Poland and overrun by Russian troops. Red Army soldiers looted the towns, torched the farms, and assaulted the women. They dug up the German graveyards, threw open their coffins, and ripped the jewellery from the corpses.

Sister Bettina poured more tea into our cups. "That summer, nine or ten million Germans were herded out of Silesia. Like worthless dogs. Losing everything. Family members far and wide scattered. Over all of Germany. East and West."

Sister lifted her cup to her lips and took long draughts of milky tea. "The Russian soldiers were barbaric peasants," she said. "Never had they seen electric lights. And water flowing out of indoor pipes at the turning of a handle? That was sorcery. They thought the German women were witches."

I shook my head. "I had no idea. We never learned about Silesia in school."

Sister took a deep breath and let it out slowly through pursed lips. "We Germans lost the war, so our expulsion didn't make it to your history books."

Before breaking the silence lying heavily between us, I gave Sister a moment to dab her mouth and eyes with a linen serviette.

"Where..." I moistened my embarrassed tongue with a hasty gulp from my cup. "Where did Sister Agatha end up?"

"With her mother she escaped. To the West. But the details I do not know. She doesn't share them. When she entered the convent she took the name Agatha, after the saint who is protecting women in danger."

Sister Bettina drained her cup and placed it gently on the tea tray. She looked over her shoulder as though to be sure we were still alone.

"Even after thirty years," she said quietly, "Sister Agatha's demonic memories are not far below the surface hidden. Behind her rigid manner, still she hides."

Yes, I mused silently, hidden like a spiny sea urchin, inside a shell that prickles as keenly as it protects.

12

Charms

Late one afternoon, Louise strutted home to our garden, a muddle of chicks tripping behind her.

I had my hand on the garden hose, flushing grit and slime from two cone shells and a gold-lipped oyster – three beauties for my collection. Louise pecked at the sandy dirt by the house and squawked at finding nothing worth swallowing. I shook a plate of rice and smiled as fuzzy bodies tumbled after the tossed leftovers.

The garden gate creaked on its hinge and clunked shut.

I turned towards the slap of flip-flops on my walkway. "Ah, Joseph," I said. "*Apinun tru.*"

I'd only ever seen him work the night shift. The sunshine on his face seemed to unsettle him, like a mole blinded by daylight.

"I suppose they need me in the men's ward."

"It Isaak, Dokta. Brother belong me. He *bigpela* sick."

"What's wrong?"

"*Bigpela* fever. Two weeks now. Every day getting higher."

Joseph snapped a branch off a guava tree and absently shredded each leaf into fragments.

"Has he had any treatment?" I asked.

"Yes, Dokta," Joseph replied. "Aid-post *dokta-boy* give him chloroquine and penicillin. For one week. Still he *bigpela sick*."

Every village had an aid-post the size of an outdoor privy, and about as spotless. *Dokta-boys* dispensed chloroquine for fevers that might be malaria, aspirin for toothaches, and penicillin for everything else. Patients who didn't improve after a couple of days were supposed to be sent to a hospital. They didn't always make it.

"Where's your brother now?"

"In Men's Ward. He come yesterday from our village. He too weak to drink. The nurses put up a drip."

I tried to get Joseph to tell me details of his brother's illness on our walk to the men's ward, but he stayed three paces behind, almost mute. All I could discover was that Isaak was a catechist in the Baining Ranges. That meant he hiked from village to village on a monthly circuit, hefting Catholicism's do's and don'ts to the Baining people who lived inland across the mountains.

Father Barrow had told me once, after slurping back several beers in the priests' mess at Vunapope, that coastal Tolai warriors had spent centuries hunting down and feasting on – the Bainings. Now scattered within the misty jungles of the interior ranges, Baining tribesfolk scrounged their existence from semi-cultivated roots, wild birds, and occasional opossums. No fish, no coconuts, little sunlight, and a day's trek to reach the nearest road.

Joseph stopped near the men's ward. He looked about as if making sure no one was in earshot, then whispered: "The Bainings in Arabam; a sickness come to their village. Last month, many people dead." He put his hand in front of his mouth and looked again from side to side. "They say a Tumbuan spreading magic."

"But Joseph ... What sort of sickness?"

"*Bigpela* fever. Eyes like death, tongues like leather, *pekpek* blood. Isaak, he saw them. He afraid. He sleep in Baining houses. Now he sick too." A pause. "Don't tell Sister. She get angry. Jesus say no talk about Tumbuans."

We found Isaak in the men's ward, lying on his back with a sheet pulled up to his chin. Beads of sweat glistened on his forehead, and his teeth chattered mechanically. He managed a rueful lift of his eyebrows, but he didn't stir.

A white-haired man stood at the foot of Isaak's bed. He clutched a small book between stiff, arthritic fingers. His white shirt gleamed; his crisp grey *laplap* boasted tailored pockets.

"Good afternoon, Dokta," he said in the raspy breaths of an asthmatic not far from an acute attack. "Good to see you again."

I swung my canvas satchel off my shoulder, groped inside it for my stethoscope, and nodded at the gentleman. "Are you one of Isaak's ... No, it can't be..."

His face opened in a huge smile. "Yes, Dokta. Michael Toliman." He touched the spot on his chest where I'd plunged the needle and snatched him back to life. "Remember?"

"You look great, Michael."

"Thank you, but it's Isaak I worry about. A sickness brought from the Bainings."

I examined Isaak from his scalp to his toenails but could find no ready cause for his fever. Apathetic resignation glazed his face, as though he'd relinquished all hope of getting better. I flipped through his bedside chart. The nurses had recorded his high temperatures and unhurried heart rates; Janet had reported no malaria in his blood smear.

High fevers, a sluggish pulse, an apathetic face. Perhaps he had typhoid fever, a contagious condition that would explain the fevers and deaths in the Baining villages.

Joseph pressed so close that I could smell the sharpness of betel nut on his breath. "What sickness he got? You make him better? Please, Dokta. I ..."

"He's got an infection. I think it's in his blood. But not malaria. I'll ask Miss Janet to do a special blood test. Then we'll start an antibiotic. Chloramphenicol." I coiled my stethoscope into my satchel. "But I expect this fever to last another week or more, before it breaks."

Joseph pursed his lips and sucked in a whistle. Michael closed his eyes and made the sign of the cross. I fingered the charm in my satchel – a dome of stippled glass I'd spotted on the beach. I'd gauged its heft and soothing texture in my palm: probably the base of a

149

champagne bottle. I imagined it tossed overboard by Captain Cooke or stolen from Captain Bligh, then fractured, etched, and polished by rocks, waves, and sand. I'd tucked it into my satchel. For good luck.

I washed my hands, insisted that everyone else do the same so they wouldn't catch Isaak's sickness, and strode to the lab to ask Janet to culture his stool and blood. If my diagnosis were correct, there'd soon be colonies of typhoid dotting Janet's Petri dishes.

By the end of the week, Isaak's fever had broken and Janet had isolated typhoid bacteria from all of his specimens. Joseph and Michael wore big smiles. Isaak threw off his bed sheet like a chick hatching from its shell. He sat cross-legged on his bed dispensing animated wisdom and drawing pictures in the air with long fingers.

By the end of the same week, Father Schiermann had brought four Baining people to Vunapope from the village of Arabam. All had fever, dehydration, and apathetic countenances. We found typhoid bacteria in their blood. That made five adults with typhoid fever, and tales of others in prior weeks. An epidemic.

Sister Pirmina summoned me to her office.

"This is serious, Dokta. An epidemic in Arabam and one of our finest catechists struck down."

"Isaak is a lot better now, Sister."

"Yes, thanks God." She patted the silver cross pinned to the bodice of her habit. "But we cannot keep putting our staff at risk. Every four weeks we are sending our nurses there to do an outreach clinic. They are the whole day spending in Arabam in close contact with the people. And their lunch eating beside the primary school. We must as soon as possible discover the cause of the epidemic."

"It could be the water supply," I said.

She shook her head. "No. They're getting all their water from the river, a long way down the mountain from the village. No pipes. Every litre carried by hand. Nearby, no other villages. Father Schiermann always says Arabam has the freshest water because the river flows so fast. You will be seeing that with your own eyes."

"What's that, Sister?"

"I am sending you on patrol to Arabam the day after tomorrow.

150

Sister Agatha will make the monthly visit with her team. You will go along. You *must* put a stop to the epidemic."

"Sister Agatha? I thought she..."

"Sister Agatha has regained her strength and her composure. She is again in charge of our community clinics. In this fine effort she has much experience." Sister Pirmina looked towards the door and stood up. "It is a walk of two hours from the end of the road to the village of Arabam. The trail it is slippery." She looked down at my flip-flops and raised her nose in disgust. "You must wear proper shoes, that just belongs to it."

Two days later I arose in the dark and joined the expedition already gathering in the glare of the lampposts outside the hospital's main entrance. Four trainee nurses had hauled several large wooden boxes out of a storage locker and arranged them on the tarmac. A Papua New Guinean nun, in the full habit of a sister who has taken her final vows, examined the contents of each box. She pleaded with the trainees to *please* stay out of trouble by fetching the rest of the gear before Sister Agatha arrived with the truck and got angry that everything wasn't ready.

"Good morning, Dokta," the young woman said, almost dancing towards me. "I'm Sister Marilyn." She launched a giggle and put her open palm over her mouth.

"Good morning to you, Sister," I said, enthralled by her crystalline eyes and innocently sensuous smile. She was a sinuous vision of polished mahogany swathed in crisp cotton.

"You're going to Arabam, too, Sister?" I asked, trying to control the eagerness in my voice.

"Oh yes," she said. "For the past year I've been going on clinic patrol as preparation for my posting to my home province. West New Britain. I will be taking charge of a health centre." She glanced at the stainless steel watch on her slender wrist. "Oh goodness! Sister Agatha will arrive any minute with the Land Cruiser. Excuse me, I must check the vaccine cooler."

While Sister Marilyn scrutinized the growing pile of patrol gear, she gave instructions with feigned impatience. From her face radiated a lightness of spirit, and I wondered if it reflected her liberation, her certainty that her family could never sell her into marital servitude in return for a handsome *brideprice*.

I stooped to study the large, scuffed boxes on the tarmac. They'd been crafted from choice rosewood, their dovetail joints fashioned by hand. Stamped inside the lids: Made at Catholic Mission Vunapope.

One box was crammed with ointments, medicines, and syringes. I was puzzling why another was packed with packets of tea, sugar, matches, and lengths of cotton when I heard the cough and rumble of an approaching vehicle.

The driver came to a halt, flung open the door, and jumped from the box-shaped jeep. She marched across the tarmac, her skirts swirling above her ankles. She'd traded her hospital whites for jungle-trek blue.

"To Arabam is a long way and the road is difficult," Sister Agatha said. "If we are to return to Vunapope by nightfall, we must get going."

"Girls! Girls!" she shouted over my shoulder. "Remember properly to pack those boxes into the truck! There was yesterday a terrible mess when that one box tipped over on the Vunakanau Hill. Sister Marilyn, I hope you have prepared the vaccine cooler."

Sister Agatha caught sight of two bananas poking from under the flap of my satchel.

"Oh Dokta!" she scoffed. "You do not need to bring your lunch. At Arabam we are giving you lunch." And, I imagined, a dose of typhoid along with it.

As soon as the nurses had stowed all the gear, the seven of us jumped into the vehicle. Sister revved the engine to a roar, and we lumbered into the watery yellow of the dawn.

Sister Agatha proved to be an expert driver. She headed inland at high speed on a paved surface that soon gave way to well-graded gravel and an easy crossing of the first ridge of coastal hills.

Twenty minutes later, she jerked the truck to a dead stop, shifted into four-wheel-drive with a ceremonial clunk, and turned onto a trail that faced a rampart of green peaks, the Baining Ranges.

We crawled into the jungle, in first gear, along two faint lines of tire tracks. The foliage pressed in like the walls of a prickly tunnel. The jeep bounced across potholes with the violence of a dinghy rocked by a heavy gale. The pitching rammed my head against the ceiling where a row of rivets jabbed my scalp. When the vegetation thinned, I realized we were climbing a crest barely wider than the vehicle. Gullies plunged to the right and left.

On a stretch of mud, the engine whined a new note. It sounded anxious, and belched blue clouds of oily smoke. The tires whirred and screamed. They'd lost their traction and were nudging us in a sideways skid towards the edge of the cliff. I braced for a nosedive down the mountain and pictured my mother standing on her doorstep, a telegram in her trembling hands, her face wet and crumpled.

I stared through the windshield, every muscle rigid, the bitter smell of rubber scorching my throat. Sister Agatha gripped the steering wheel with her beefy hands, clenched her tongue between her teeth, and aimed at a patch of solid ground. The front wheels caught a bed of stones and the jeep lurched back onto the trail. Sister Agatha flashed a grin, Sister Marilyn clapped her hands, and I drew in huge gulps of air.

Before I had confidence enough to release my grip on the dashboard, we rounded a bend and came to a halt. Ahead of us, the track vanished into a gash a couple of meters wide and just as deep. There was no way we could cross, and we couldn't abandon the jeep on this razor-edge ridge.

Was Sister Agatha going to reverse the Land Cruiser all the way down that murderous trail? I grabbed the door handle; ready to leap out the instant Sister shoved the gear lever into reverse. I would hike through the ruts and mud, all the way to Vunapope if necessary. But Sister didn't touch the gear lever; she killed the engine.

The nurses opened their doors and stepped confidently into the underbrush. They returned with roots, logs, and stones, and we repaired the crater with the skill of a well-practised road crew. Fifteen minutes later, Sister eased the Land Cruiser over our improvised roadbed.

After a further half-hour of pitching, roaring, grinding, and the reek of our sweaty bodies roasting in the overheated cab, a thatched hut emerged from the jungle at the end of the track. Sister sounded the horn and turned off the ignition. My head throbbed, my ears rang, and my shoulders dropped in relief. The unruffled stillness was sublime, but short-lived.

Four short Baining men appeared from the undergrowth, their muscular bodies clad only in dark *laplaps,* the printed patterns obscured by years of grime and mud. Their conspicuous brows, woolly beards, and blackened teeth formed prehistoric faces that seemed incapable of humour. They quickly extracted the gear from the Land Cruiser and stacked onto their heads and shoulders the four rosewood boxes, three folding tables, two burlap sacks, and the vaccine cooler. Puffing cigarettes rolled from forest leaves, they carried the load over the ridges to Arabam with the confident precision of circus performers.

Our path took us through bush so thick it swallowed everything and everyone more than three or four paces beyond me. Stands of tall hardwoods, intertwined with massive vines, produced a canopy that cast us in twilight. Raw and cheeky banter echoed from the invisible treetops. Cockatoos, the nurses said.

I felt, but could not see, the incline as we headed down the mountainside. The steep, mucky foot-trail called for constant concentration, and I was slower than the others. I tripped over roots and stones, and fell down hard on my backside when my sturdy but inadequate running shoes slid out from under me.

My companions, except for Sister Agatha, walked barefoot on splayed-out feet well adapted to the terrain. Layers of callus protected their soles and promoted painless tramping over the sharpest stones and prickliest vines. They gripped roots and rocks with their thumb-like toes and never made a false step. The Baining men, our boxes and tables atop their heads, descended the trail as if it were a carpeted staircase.

The tentacles of the forest lashed at my face. Plaques of mud and clay, contracting on my skin, itched like scores of mosquito bites. My light canvas satchel strained at my shoulder like an infantryman's overloaded rucksack. I thought of Arthur Hadley-Rix, the coast

154

watcher, scrambling up and down these ranges during WWII: heavy gear on his back, starvation rations in his stomach, malaria in his bloodstream, and Japanese soldiers on his tail. Arthur had survived three years. One hour of this flogging was about to finish me. Just as I thought I could stand the ordeal no longer, the path opened onto the bank of a wide and sleepy river.

Our little band assembled at the water's edge. The two sisters conferred with the Baining carriers, pointing here and there at shoals and boulders in the current. I looked up and down for a footbridge that would take us the seventy-five meters across the water. No bridge. I looked for a rowboat. No rowboat. Not even a makeshift raft.

One of the men, a box and table still balanced on his head, waded into the river. The water swirled to his mid-chest. He looked content, his load secure. The three other carriers ambled behind him, coils of smoke twirling from their cigarettes.

Sister Agatha stepped off the bank. The brown water swallowed her skirts.

"Come, Dokta," she called from the river. "The vater ist vonderful." She splashed her face. "Loft-ly unt cool."

I set my jaw, forced notions of crocodiles from my head, and waded in, clutching my satchel high and dry above my head. The cool water brought immediate relief to my prickled skin, but the current's thrust was far heavier than the peaceful surface had promised. Every step was a delicate balancing act. Halfway across I tripped over a slimy object on the riverbed. Two students, yet to say a word since leaving Vunapope, grabbed me by the shoulders, saving me, my lunch, and my satchel from an uncertain fate. When I regained my balance, the nurses giggled and stayed closer than my shadow while we inched to the other side.

Then began the breath-stealing clamber out of the valley, up another trail of mud and treachery. The air was so hot that our clothes dried quickly. Sister Agatha kept pace with the swift Baining carriers. Sister Marilyn gave smiles and encouragement from a few steps ahead of me. By the time we reached the summit of the track and the end of my ordeal, I was drunk with heat, thirst, and exhaustion. But thanks to the students who steadied my uncertain footfalls with their brawny hands, I was still standing.

Arabam turned out to be a few dozen huts and a rustic schoolhouse on a sleepy plateau. To my relief, the place looked almost deserted. No throngs of people languishing with fever. No corpses piled high. No stalls serving food laced with typhoid. Just kids no more than five years old, darting through the mud, their infant siblings riding on their backs.

I dropped to the ground, guzzled a litre of water, and ate my bananas. A distant panorama of jagged peaks poked into clouds that hovered in the intense blue sky. The scenery was postcard-perfect, but the village crude and colourless. The scattered dwellings looked sadly temporary, their walls no more substantial than mats woven from cane and pandanus leaves. Wisps of smoke meandered through roofs thatched with brittle leaves.

The nuns and nurses unfolded their tables and set them on the grass. They unpacked the boxes and suspended a grocer's scale from the branch of a tall tree. A young man shuffled towards us clutching a triton, a spotted seashell about the size of a football. He wore a shirt with buttons, and not a *laplap*, but a pair of shorts.

"Here comes Peter," Sister Marilyn said. "He's the primary school teacher." Again, that radiant smile of freedom. "He comes from West New Britain, just like me. We're *wantoks*."

As clansmen, they shared "one talk", the tribal language of their home district.

"Did Isaak get to Vunapope?" Peter asked. "He was very sick. I worry about him."

"Dokta has come to find out about the sickness," Sister Agatha said. "Some detective work."

"Isaak's getting better. He'll be okay," I said. "It was typhoid fever. Those people Father Schiermann brought from here last week? They had it too. Do you know of any new cases?"

"One woman had fever but I gave her chloroquine and it went away."

"Peter is also the *dokta-boy* here," Sister Marilyn said, clearly proud of her *wantok*.

"Have you had any celebrations here lately?" I asked. "Weddings? A big feast?" A large group sharing a contaminated meal was the most likely source of the typhoid outbreak.

"No," Peter said. "No wedding or *singsing* for a long time. And no *mumu*." He rolled his eyes. "Coconuts don't grow up here. Too far from the sea."

Coastal people loved their *mumu*: meat and vegetables simmered in coconut cream. Thinking of it made my mouth water.

Sister Marilyn put her hand into a *bilum* and pulled out a ripe coconut. "A present for you, *Wantok*. But first you must blow your trumpet. We're ready to start the clinic."

Peter eyed the coconut hungrily, and pursed his lips over a hole in the side of the triton. He blew the shell like a bugle, and the piercing blast echoed from the hillsides.

Within a few minutes, mothers and children formed a line in front of our earnest-faced nursing students gathered at two tables. The two senior students supervised the two juniors, and Sister Marilyn acted as a consultant for problem cases. Sister Agatha left them to their tasks with a minimum of interference.

The first of some seventy children seen that day was a boy about two years old. He was identified by name and his record, a yellow card, was pulled from a box. A nurse plunked him in a small hammock attached to the grocery scale. He screamed and bounced in the scary contraption, and the indicator needle oscillated wildly. The nurses argued over the reading and scrutinized his dog-eared card. The nurse with the loudest voice settled on the weight, recorded it, and decided he was due for a vaccine injection.

The next child in line was a girl just old enough to walk. She underwent the same procedure with the yellow card, the weighing contraption, and injection. As well, a nurse dipped a cotton rag in a bottle of dark purple liquid and painted every sore on the girl's legs.

"The Bainings love that gentian violet," said Sister Marilyn. "Doesn't do much for sores, but the bright purple stays on a week. Sister Agatha calls it a memento of our visit. It brings mothers to the clinic and they let us vaccinate children, everyone is happy."

The Vunapope clinic was obviously a highlight in the life of the community. While the women gossiped in the lengthening queue, the men watched from a distance, arms folded, faces sober, crimson betel nut dripping from their mouths. Babies screeched and spluttered as the nurses forced malaria tablets down their throats. Adolescent boys with infected cuts stood stoically for injections of long-lasting penicillin.

Concentric lines and sweeping whorls adorned the skin of almost everyone. It seemed an enthusiastic tattoo artist had honed his technique in this village where people wore hardly any clothing, just *laplaps*. Each finely drawn pattern was much the same as the others. But a closer look revealed not tattoos, but some sort of scaly skin disease.

Sister Marilyn saw me examining the markings on one boy's chest. "It's a type of ringworm," she said. "They call it *grilly*. All the Bainings have it. They don't want us to treat it. It's itchy, but they don't care."

While the nurses conducted their medical parade, Sister Agatha drew her own crowd by the shade of a mango tree. She opened two rosewood boxes and from them sold tea, sugar, biscuits, matches, soap, thread, and lengths of cloth. With the skill of a seasoned trader at a market stall, she bartered in Pidgin and Baining tribal language. Her smiles and sparkling eyes had removed all trace of her midwife's bark and rally driver's furrowed brow.

"See all the customers at my little store? Always they are glad to see me. They are each time buying every bag of sugar. And all the biscuits." She winked and chuckled. "But not enough soap." She pointed behind me, and coins jingled in her hand. "I think Peter and Sister Marilyn have some customers for you. It is a special day in Arabam when a doctor visits."

"Excuse me, Dokta," Sister Marilyn said. "There's someone who'd like to meet you. Her name is Zanta and she is very old."

"And crippled," Peter added. "She never leaves her house."

"I think she had polio as a child," Sister Marilyn said. "She never married – no man wants a woman who cannot carry water from the river."

"But she has a memory like a picture book," Peter said. "Every new baby is brought to her so she can see it and remember its name and its parents."

They led me into the bush along a maze of footpaths. More of Arabam was hidden in the forest than was clustered in the open space around the school. We came to a windowless shack about three paces square. Bamboo poles framed its corners; strips of cane formed its woven walls. Its roof, a tangle of leaves, jutted no higher than my forehead.

Peter knocked, and we ducked through the open doorway into the dark room. A wrinkled crone, sitting propped against a wall, was grating something into an enamel bowl between her withered legs. I felt too tall, too clean, too pale inside the tiny, grimy, private space. But I forced a smile and crouched onto the dirt floor in front of the woman. Draughts of smoke, curling from a ragged heap of ash and embers, stung my eyes.

"*Apinun tru*," I said.

The woman stopped grating and put down her tool, a large flat seashell – a silver-tipped oyster, mother of pearl. She stared at my hair, my face, my satchel. She wiped her hands on her *laplap* and stroked my forearm with the tips of her knobbly fingers. She bent forward for a close inspection of the blonde hairs that sprouted from my pallid skin. Her touch felt professional, welcoming.

"*Apinun, Dokta. Name belong me, Zanta.*" She smiled and pulled at her frizzy white hair. She patted her wrinkled breasts that dangled, limp and deflated. "*Me lapun meri.*" She cackled at her joke, at having stated the obvious: she was an old woman.

Zanta reached for a tin of tobacco and knocked against a shallow pan partially hidden behind her. Something sloshed inside it and the acrid smell of urine hit my nose. Embarrassed at the close range of her sullied chamber pot, I surveyed the room while she rolled and lit a cigarette. Zanta had few possessions, not even a table. A hurricane lamp, a long-bladed knife, and a clutch of enamel dishes lay within easy reach. Her bed was a pandanus mat, a soot-stained pillow, and a crumpled *laplap*. To her right, beside three coconuts, a bilum bulged with twigs and leaves.

I leaned towards Peter, crouched beside me. "I thought you said there were no coconuts around here," I said. "Look – she's got a stash of them."

"Your carriers brought those today. She makes medicine with them. Coconut mixed with plants from the forest. No one knows exactly how she does it."

I hadn't noticed it was coconut she'd been grating with the oyster shell.

"Where did they get the coconuts?"

"From the Tolais at the end of the trail. They trade coconuts for animal skins, parrot feathers, boar's teeth."

"What's the medicine a treatment for?" I asked.

Peter looked embarrassed, and muttered to Sister Marilyn in their tribal language.

Sister giggled. "It's for married men whose wives can't give them children."

"It strengthens their seed," Peter said. He pointed to six identical glass jars arranged neatly on the floor. "That's the medicine there. Isaak brought the empty glass pots."

The squat containers were unmistakable. A plump baby beamed from labels imprinted on the metal lids. Only one jar had anything in it, a liquid that looked like milky tea. I was stunned to think this same container had held a meal for Andy Morrison, one of many Gerber dinners shipped to Vunapope from Miami because his mother was afraid he might overdose on sugar and salt.

The stench of the chamber pot loitered in my nostrils like a vulgar intruder.

"Can you ask Zanta if she boils her medicine?" I said.

The three of them had a rapid-fire discussion. I barely caught a word of their Pidgin. By the look on her face, the old woman was determined not to give up any of the secrets that guarded her potion.

Finally, Peter presented her answer. "No, she doesn't boil it. She doesn't need to. It works fine without it."

"And she's short of firewood," Sister Marilyn added.

"Did Isaak drink any of Zanta's medicine?" I asked.

"He bought the last jar she had," Peter said. "He told me she made him pay double for it, but it was worth it to have a baby."

"Married three years and still his wife has not been blessed with a child," Sister said.

"I think the typhoid is coming from the medicine," I said. "That chamber pot is probably full of typhoid germs. They'll be all over her hands. And her tools."

Sister Marilyn gasped and looked at her own hands.

Peter's eyes bulged as if he were about to vomit.

Then it hit me: Zanta had spread typhoid on my forearm when she explored it with her fingers. I held my breath.

The three of us backed out through the doorway, dusted Zanta's dirt from our clothes, and stared at each other.

"We've got to get her to boil the medicine before she gives it to anyone else," I said, holding my arms against my thighs, as far from my mouth as possible.

"She's a stubborn old woman," Peter said. "She's not going to change how she makes her medicine."

"Older people don't believe in germs," Sister Marilyn said. "She'll laugh if we tell her that germs are jumping into the medicine from her bedpan."

"Does she believe in spirits?" I asked.

"Yes," Peter nodded. "The Bainings say spirits control all."

"Can we tell her that the Tolais put evil spirits in the coconuts?" I asked. "Evil spirits that can only be removed by boiling the medicine?"

"She might not believe boiling is strong enough," Sister Marilyn said uneasily.

Peter nodded in agreement: "She might want a power-stone – a secret charm she can bury in the fire to give it the force to destroy evil. But it must be something special. Not just a rock from the river or a feather from the forest."

I slipped my hand into my satchel. Should I show them my glass charm? It fit my palm so perfectly, its touch so soothing. Could

I part with it? If I were honest, its power was imagined. But in the Baining Ranges, a piece of glass plucked from the beach, and buried beneath a cooking fire, had life-saving power. If I kept it, the glass wouldn't feel lucky in my satchel. It would feel evil. "How about something from the sea?" I asked.

Their eyes grew huge at the sight of the bottle-green dome in my palm. They explored its stippled surface with their fingers, and marvelled as it glowed in the sunlight. The perfect power-stone for Zanta's fire. We agreed to keep our contaminated fingers away from our mouths, ducked through the door, and crouched gingerly once more on the dirt in front of Zanta.

Peter explained about the coconuts, the bad spirits, the catechist and others sick with fever, the need to boil the medicine.

Zanta's face screwed up with anger. She hurled a coconut through the doorway.

When she grabbed another, I produced the charm from my pocket. Peter extolled its virtues.

The old woman squinted, dropped the coconut, and cackled in amazement. She took the orb as delicately as an art dealer handling a Fabergé Egg.

She turned it over, held it up to a sunbeam streaking through the doorway, and rubbed it against her cheek. It was the only coloured thing in her sooty cabin.

Yes, she would hide it under her fire. She'd destroy the Tolai's evil magic. She'd boil every batch of medicine, and pour it, steaming hot, into the little glass pots. The spirits of the happy babies would guard the potion.

Zanta reached under her *laplap,* retrieved a string of rosary beads, and held it high. "A present from Isaak," she said, in Pidgin. "I'm going to talk to Jesus. Tell him to send Isaak back to our place, and bless his wife with a baby."

She cradled the glass dome in her palm, looped the rosary through her fingers, and lifted its crucifix to her lips; then she bowed her head and closed her eyes.

13

Buttons

This was no time for half measures. I plunged the entire vial of Valium into the child's vein.

Cora-Lee's body relaxed on the treatment table like a sparrow landing on a safe branch and folding its wings.

My heart hammered a frantic cadence against my ribs. Air buzzed back and forth across the girl's cherry lips and baby teeth.

I didn't move. I couldn't dare to.

Sweat trickled down my neck. My back, still black and blue, ached where the rocks had bashed my flesh on the slippery trail to Arabam and back again.

If I didn't flicker a muscle, maybe Cora-Lee's convulsions wouldn't return, wouldn't clench her limbs, her throat, her spine in another death grip.

Maybe her heart would echo mine and keep pounding, pumping for her life.

Cora-Lee's cracked lips, sunken eyes and enveloping stench told a too-familiar story.

She'd been carried into Children's Ward minutes earlier, withered and unconscious after too many days of diarrhea. The nurses set up an intravenous and called for me. The dose of fluid had strengthened her pulse, they said.

I arrived to watch Cora stirring from her coma. She looked into my face. She blinked.

Then, like five other dehydrated toddlers who'd died here under my hands, she rolled her eyeballs upward, leered a grimace, and raised her arms, stiff as driftwood sticks.

Her rigid legs and spine arched like a tightly drawn bow. Her breathing ceased, her heartbeat would be next.

Desperate for a drug to drive the asphyxiating spasms from her muscles, I'd wanted to shout for an ampoule of Valium.

But would the sedative propel her into deeper shock? Would it stun her heart and brain with too harsh a blow?

On the other frenzied occasions I'd been too timid to risk the Valium; but after five deaths, I couldn't just stand and brace for the certainty of harrowing wails, of funereal keening from the anguished throats of the little girl's family. I'd grabbed the syringe and shot in the drug.

The minute-hand crawled through a quarter hour on the clock in Children's Ward. I took a deep breath, stepped back, and rubbed my face with my shirttail.

Cora-Lee didn't flinch. Her lips held their rosy colour.

"Okay, Edwina. The Valium seems to be working." My voice sounded like an explosion after so many minutes of silence. "You can take her pulse and blood pressure now."

Edwina, the Tolai nurse in charge of Children's Ward, had been as rooted to the floor as I had. She cast a worried frown.

"Yes, I think we're okay." I pointed to a cupboard. "But pass me another vial of Valium. I'll hold it just in case."

An hour later, Cora-Lee lay relaxed in slumber. Her intravenous dripped smoothly, and the pulse in her neck thumped with confidence.

For half a minute her arms had stiffened again in what looked like a prelude of worse to come, but a quarter-dose of Valium settled

Cora-Lee's overheated muscles and my momentary wave of panic.

Lillianna and the other dehydrated children who'd convulsed and died in identical scenarios had been wrapped in *laplap* shrouds, then swept away so quickly that I'd never caught more than scanty details about their illnesses.

This time I peppered Edwina with questions.

She squeezed answers from the broad-hipped Tolai woman trembling beside the table: Cora-Lee's grandmother.

The two women spoke in their tribal language, the grandmother blurting monosyllables between sobs and tears, while I pressed for details.

"Ask if the child received her proper immunizations."

"Yes," Edwina answered. "They live in Paparatava village, next to the health centre."

The spasms looked like tetanus, but Cora-Lee couldn't have lockjaw. Sister Robin made sure every child received every shot, including tetanus.

"Has she had fits or spasms like this before?" I asked.

The grandmother stared into Edwina's face, then shook her head and dabbed her tears in the cabbage roses printed on the shiny polyester of her *meri-blouse*.

"Did anyone give her medicine?" I asked.

The woman looked over her shoulder, then at the large string bag, the *bilum*, at her feet. She covered her mouth with her hands and mumbled a response.

The look of confidence evaporated from Edwina's face.

She bit her lower lip. "Nothing. Well, nothing from the pharmacy."

"What are you saying, Edwina?"

"I don't know."

"What do you mean, *you don't know*?" I demanded.

Edwina looked over towards two student nurses counting pills and rolling bandages, then stared absently at the clear solution dripping into Cora-Lee's intravenous line.

"Please, Edwina," I insisted. "There's something you don't want to tell me, isn't there?"

"Yes."

"Is it about some sort of medicine?"

"Yes."

"Did the grandmother give her something?"

"Maybe."

"Can you find out?"

With a sharp hiss and a flick of her hand Edwina shooed three bystanders and the two student nurses out of the treatment room. She pointed to the *bilum* and directed the grandmother to bring it to a far corner. After a few moments, the woman burst into wails while Edwina returned clutching something in her fist.

Edwina opened her hand. There, on a crumpled strip of banana leaf, lay three grey-green velvet buttons. One of them had been cracked into pieces. Buttons! I picked up a fragment, fingered it, and lifted it towards my face.

"Dokta!" Edwina's face filled with alarm. "Don't taste it."

I shut my mouth, pressed my lips together, and sniffed. No smell. I looked closer. It wasn't a button. It was a seed. The same kind I'd found in the hair of the dehydrated girl who'd stiffened and died in my freshman month at Vunapope. That was one year, thousands of patients, and countless sessions of CPR ago.

I turned to Edwina: "What is it?"

"Bush medicine," she answered.

"What did she do with it?"

"Made a powder."

"And then what?"

Edwina stared at Cora-Lee. She fiddled with the barrettes at the back of her nurse's cap. She looked back at the grandmother, crouched and sobbing in the corner.

I was losing my patience: "And then what, Edwina?"

"She put some on the girl's tongue while they drove here."

"Why?"

"To wake her up. Make her heart beat stronger. She was afraid. She thought the child would die before they got here."

I shook my head, then asked: "What's it called?"

Edwina shrugged. "Just bush medicine. Seeds from a plant." A deep breath. A guilty look. "My auntie keeps hers in a tin box. For her weak heart."

I swallowed hard, then asked: "How does she take it?"

"Puts a few grains of powder under her tongue. She says more than half a seed is poisonous."

Poisonous! The word echoed loudly in my mind. I looked at Cora-Lee, snoring rhythmically on the table. What was the poison stalking her veins? Was it digitalis, the potent heart drug extracted from foxglove flowers?

Even a modest overdose of digitalis could be lethal. It caused convulsions and stopped the heart. Our professors in medical school had lectured us *ad nauseam*, insisting we calculate *exactly* the right dose for every patient. Base the dose on body weight, they said. Smaller doses for smaller people.

That was it! Well-meaning relatives had given those kids digitalis to strengthen their heartbeats, but had given too much.

My spinster aunt grew foxglove in her Hampshire flower garden: trumpet blossoms on tall stalks. I'd seen them when I'd spent a weekend at her cluttered cottage in England. She called them *dead man's thimbles*.

"Hard to believe a miracle drug is sunning itself in my garden," Aunt Bet had said.

Why hadn't I discovered this before? Why did so many kids have to die before I figured it out? I'd intended to examine those first broken seeds I'd found, but left them in my shorts pocket in a pile of clothes in my bedroom. Rosa laundered them to oblivion. I'd never seen anything like those broken bits again. Until today.

I placed the seeds on Sister Leora's pharmacy counter.

"Can you tell me what these are, Sister? Are they some kind of bush medicine?"

She pulled a magnifying glass from her apron pocket and inspected the velvety buttons. "No, I've never seen anything like those before. Mind you, I'm no expert when it comes to bush medicine." She pointed to a shelf crowded with bottles of her famous cough medicine. "Got my hands full of my own potions."

I felt as crushed as the broken seed on the counter. "Are you sure, Sister? Have another look. Is it foxglove? I mean digitalis?"

"I know what you mean, Doc, but as far as I know there's no foxglove in these parts. Sun's too strong."

She pulled off her spectacles and massaged the lenses with her hankie. "Years ago, someone sent Sister Camilla some seeds from Germany. I'm pretty sure they were foxglove. Sprouted but soon withered away. The only digitalis I know of around here comes as proper pills."

"Does Sister Camilla live at Vunapope?"

"Yes, she's still here. Lives in our convent."

"Can you help me ask her to look at these? Maybe she'll remember if they look like her foxglove seeds?"

"A waste of time, Doc. Sister Camilla's gone all senile. Doesn't even remember her own name, poor thing."

Sister Leora tucked her magnifying glass back into her apron and lifted a jar of tablets from a shelf behind her.

"Maybe you just better stick to what you know best," she said. "Like your special milk formula. That really has taken off like Grant through our beloved Confederate capital."

She tucked the large plastic jar under her arm and winced as she twisted its lid with her gnarled, arthritic fingers.

"I've got two girls volunteering from the high school... taught 'em how to measure out the ingredients," she grunted as she worked the lid. "They come twice a week after school so's I don't get behind on my orders from Children's Ward."

With that, she poured a heap of white tablets onto a counting tray, adjusted her spectacles, and smiled. "Must be a lot of plump little pikininis returnin' to their villages thanks to that VSF stuff you came up with."

Sister had been a great sport about the VSF. Her enthusiasm seemed boundless and spurred perhaps by her antipathy to the imperious Sister Pirmina, who still let it be known that she didn't approve of the milk-as-medicine idea.

I folded the seeds into their banana leaf wrapper, stuffed the poisonous orphans into my satchel, thanked Sister Leora for her trouble, and shuffled out of the pharmacy. It was a terrible letdown that Sister's pharmaceutical expertise and vivacity didn't extend to the rainforest. Would another year go by without an answer?

"Doc! Doc!" Sister Leora suddenly called through the open doorway. "Now I remember. The high school. Not the one at Vunapope, but the government school in Kokopo. That young teacher from Canada – what's her name?"

"You mean Dawna Wallis?"

"Yes, that's it. Mrs. Dawna. She might recognize those seeds. She was here the other day. Had some questions about medicinal leaves and flowers. To tell you the truth, I wasn't much help. She knew a lot more than me."

"What did she ask you about?"

"Examples of herbal cures and poisons. For her botany class. Wanted to keep things exciting for her students." Sister chuckled. "Especially with talk about poisons, I reckon."

Maybe it was more exciting – and relevant – than she knew.

Later that afternoon, as the sun adjusted its burners from turbo-charged to simmer in anticipation of its daily crash into the sea, I pulled up to Garnet and Dawna's house-on-stilts in Kokopo.

"Hi Ross, what's up?" Dawna called from the top of the steps. "Garnet's at the golf club. Fixing a sprinkler. You're just in time for herbal tea and johnnycake."

I took the stairs two at a time. The air at the top was gravid with the sweet, comforting aroma of something pulled fresh from the oven. "Garnet sure is lucky to be married to a dietician," I said.

Dawna pointed to her tummy, bulging with pregnancy. "Gotta do my best to look after Junior, eh? No beer, no caffeine. Lots of fruit, protein, and vitamins."

For all her good humour and rich smile, gestational puffiness had distorted Dawna's cheeks; exhaustion had turned her sprightly steps into waddles.

"It must be tough being pregnant in this heat," I said. "Only eight more weeks to go?"

She rolled her eyes. "Ten weeks and two days. And not a second longer, even if I have to drink an entire bottle of castor oil to kick-start the labour pains. My golf swing is off something fierce."

Dawna placed two plates on the kitchen table, each adorned with a golden piece of johnnycake.

I pulled the banana leaf envelope from my satchel and spread its contents on the table. "Speaking of home remedies," I said, "do you know what these are?"

"Sure," she shrugged. "They're *nux vomica* seeds."

"Nooks vomit what?"

She laughed. "Vaw-mi-cah, not vomit. *Nux vomica*, the dog button plant."

"What's it for?"

"Poisoning rats. And enemies, I suppose. It's strychnine."

"Strychnine!" I could feel the blood drain from my face. I steadied myself with both hands pressed on the table.

"Yep," Dawna continued, apparently oblivious to my reaction, "it grows in the bush all over New Britain. It's a small tree that's hard to spot in the rainforest behind the creeping vines. I've got pictures of it in one of my books."

She pulled a plastic bag from a drawer.

"But first, drop that stuff inside here," she advised. "And go wash your hands. Just a trace of the powder from those seeds might be poisonous."

She lifted our untouched plates from the table and flicked the two cubes of johnnycake into the garbage can. "It causes a horrible death – every muscle in the body goes rigid and the heart stops."

When I returned from the bathroom, smelling of soap from my elbows to my fingertips, two new pieces of johnnycake beamed at me from the table, which was covered with a fresh tablecloth. Dawna had her fingers pressed to the page of an open book.

She pointed to a detailed line drawing. "Here it is. *Nux vomica*, source of strychnine."

The seeds etched on the page in black and white matched exactly what lay wrapped in plastic and stuffed in my pocket.

"My God, that's spooky," I said, feeling faint.

I stared beyond the page and saw again the parched, fragile bodies convulsing on the table in Children's Ward; the wails of anguished families echoed in my ears.

"Where did you get those seeds from?" Dawna asked. "Ross... Ross, are you okay? Here, have a glass of ice water."

Between gulps, I told Dawna about Cora-Lee and her grandmother; about the other kids who must have been poisoned the same way.

Dawna stroked her swollen belly with a motherly hand. "Oh my God. That's awful, Ross. For you, and for them."

She took several draughts from her chamomile tea, and dabbed the mist of sweat from her forehead with a tissue.

"I've been struggling with how to introduce my biology class to the dangers of bush medicine," she finally said with a smile. "We know so little about it, eh? You've sure shown me the place to start."

Driving back to the hospital, I puzzled over the sequence of events surrounding the poisonings. Why hadn't the children died before they reached us?

Why had they only begun to show signs of strychnine ingestion *after* we'd started treating them? What were we doing wrong?

I found Cora-Lee fast asleep in Children's Ward, a bare light bulb hanging on a cord above her crib, a ragged scapula of the Sacred Heart suspended from a thread around her neck. Her lips glistened with newfound moisture.

Her grandmother, breasts bare and head bowed, stood grasping Cora-Lee's hand with both of hers, as though such a firm and loving clasp would prevent the girl from being pulled into the next world.

The woman looked up and smiled at me, then tears drizzled her cheeks and she turned away.

I patted the woman's forearm and gave it a squeeze. "*Cora-Lee, bai i-orait.*" Her granddaughter would recover; she'd be all right.

Watching the crystalline droplets tap their brisk rhythm into Cora-Lee's intravenous tubing, I suddenly saw the conspiracy of elements that had plotted her dehydration, her shock, and her nearly lethal spasms.

Finally, I understood why powdered strychnine didn't induce convulsions until after we filled the children's veins with our I.V. fluid.

Diarrhea – severe, prolonged, and untreated – depleted the body's fluids. Dehydration turned the tissues from plums to prunes.

Shock forced the heart to pump only a trickle of blood to the stomach, to reserve its precious flow for the body's VIPs – the brain, the heart, the kidneys.

Intravenous fluids restored the blood supply, reversed the shock, and strengthened the pulse.

But blood then rushed through the vessels of the deprived stomach, picked up the grains of bush medicine sitting there, and disbursed the lethal measure all over the body.

It would take a generation or two for Dawna Wallis's biology classes to digest and disseminate her message about the dangers of the dog button plant.

In the meantime, I'd have to teach the nurses to keep the Valium handy for every child admitted with shock and dehydration, and hope it worked as well for other kids as it had for Cora-Lee.

14

Undone

The aircraft PA system volume rose to an audible level mid-sentence: "...to start our descent into Rabaul. Please fasten your seatbelts and bring your chairs and trays into the upright position."

I peered through the oval window of the F-27 turboprop, Air Niuguini's Dutch-made draft horse.

The first time I experienced the spectacular approach that skimmed the leafy peaks of Rabaul's three volcanoes, I crumpled my boarding pass into a wad of sweaty pulp.

On today's descent over those conical beauties dozing on the rim of our enormous basin, my pulse quickened not with the strain of anxiety, but with the exhilaration of coming home. Home to the rhythm of the waves breaking on the beach; home to my bungalow and to faithful Louise pecking in my garden; home to Kokopo and my golfing buddies; home to a stimulating parade of grateful patients and to the people of New Britain whose lives touched mine with uncluttered intimacy.

We banked over the crest of Matupit. Spurts of yellow smoke puffed lazily from its stony caldera, the only sign that molten furies seethed beneath the placid turquoise waters.

A moment later, we touched down and came to a full stop.

The flight attendant opened the exit door. After two weeks vacation in the cool breezes of the New Guinea Highlands, Rabaul's warm air was so thick I felt I could cut it like pound cake.

As I crossed the black tarmac of the airfield, I welcomed the silky, lowland humidity stroking my arms; I'd missed its soothing presence in the dry mountains of the mainland.

Kent Eastman stepped out of the crowd of greeters and grasped my shoulder. "Hey Roscoe, how's it going, mate?" He pumped my hand vigorously. "Have a good holiday?"

Janet Lundquist, in her white laboratory sundress, nuzzled Kent, her arm looped through his. Their eyes, hers green, his blue, sparkled with love for each other and affection for me, as we walked to the baggage conveyer belt.

"Take lots of pictures?" Janet asked. She steadied the Nikon that seldom left its perch on the nylon strap around her neck.

"Four rolls of thirty-six," I grinned in response.

"Fantastic," she said. "Can't wait to see them."

I reached for my suitcase as it lumbered towards us on a rickety conveyor belt, but Kent's longer limbs beat me to it.

He led us across the parking lot towards his car. "Missed you on the golf course, Roscoe."

"Yeah," Janet teased. "Without you there, Kent always had Kokopo's worst score of the day."

Kent tossed my case into the trunk of his Toyota. "Steady on," he protested as we climbed into the car. "I had a couple good rounds last week."

We cruised past the royal palms lining Mango Avenue and into the smell, like home-baked cookies, that hung outside the copra factory on the road to Kokopo. They processed coconuts there – toasted the nutmeat, extracted the oil, and released the aroma that must fill every corner of Heaven. We took huge breaths, smiled and nodded, and exchanged gossip about characters at the mission.

"And how's our *dear* Sister Piranha?" I asked.

"She's okay, I guess," Janet replied. "But Sister Bettina, she's in a real state. She's..."

"Let the man enjoy the last few minutes of his holiday," Kent said. "He'll hear plenty of goings-on in Maternity, soon enough."

"What do you mean?" I said. "What *goings-on*?"

They smirked.

"Come on, you two," I implored. "Don't leave me hanging. What happened?"

"Janet knows all the gory details," Kent said. He winked at her. "Go ahead, tell him."

"Did you meet that new locum doctor from Australia?" she asked. "The one who came to cover so you could go on vacation?"

"Yeah, he arrived a week late," I said. "There was barely enough time for me to give him a half-day tour of the wards. Doctor Rudd... or was it Budd?"

Janet nodded. "Rudd. David Rudd. I heard he told Sister Piranha that he was a general practitioner – used to doing Medicine of all kinds."

"He told me that, too," I said.

"Well," Janet smirked, "his first morning in Maternity, he dropped a brand new baby."

"Yeah," Kent said. "Into a bucket-basin thing on the floor."

"It was the basin for the membranes and the afterbirth," Janet said primly.

Kent chuckled, his ears glowing pink. "The idiot didn't know a newborn baby would be slippery.

"Fortunately, the baby was okay," Janet said. "No bruises."

"Turns out the guy's been doing insurance physicals the past twenty years," Kent said, "in an office tower overlooking Sydney harbour. The closest he's been to a newborn baby is a kangaroo joey at the Taronga Park Zoo."

We burst into chortles. I felt the warm belly glow of laughter shared with friends at close range.

"You know how sweet Sister Bettina is," Janet said. "Never raises her voice. Well, she told everyone Dr. Rudd must've been born with ten thumbs. And without the sense Our Lord gave a cowrie shell. She won't let him back in her ward. She's sending every complicated delivery to Nonga, in the Vunapope ambulance."

Kent was still laughing. "Sister Pirmina is fuming. Who knows who she's madder at, Sister Bettina or Doctor Rudd."

I pictured Sister Pirmina, hands on her hips, piranha teeth flashing, mortified at watching mothers leave her beautiful Vunapope for the filthy labour ward at the government hospital.

"Both sisters are gonna be real glad you're back," Janet said.

I smiled. Sister Bettina would give me tea and shortbread, like Mrs. Tiggy-winkle.

I suspected Sister Pirmina would say nothing but her silence would speak volumes. I couldn't help but gloat at her loss of face, and I imagined her chagrin at having to pay for so many expensive ambulance trips.

I was home just long enough to drop my suitcase and head for the bathroom. The phone rang while I was drying my hands.

"Welcome back, Dokta. This is Veronika calling from Maternity. Sister asks please come at once."

"What's the ..."

The line went dead.

I flew out the door.

I found Sister Bettina gowned, gloved, and crouching between the thighs of a woman who was yelling in agony.

Breathless, Sister thanked me for coming so quickly. "I can't deliver the shoulders," she said, her voice rising, her eyes widening. "The head, it came out. But the shoulders, they are stuck."

The contraction eased. The woman moaned softly between gulps of air.

Sister glanced at Veronika who pressed her ear against a small, trumpet-like fetoscope positioned near the mother's navel. Veronika lifted her eyebrows and nodded gravely.

"Yes, the fetal heart is still beating," continued Sister, "but the infant's face by the minute it is getting bluer."

A large head jutted between its mother's bulky thighs. Slime smeared its wavy black hair, and its deep purple face grimaced like a prize-fighter, a burly boxer – lips fat and eyes bulging with determination.

The woman began to scream and shout again. I couldn't understand her tribal language, but she was clearly pleading with her sainted Mama, Papa, and Baby Jesus.

With no time to scrub, I threw on a gown and gloves. I grasped the baby's head and tried to jostle its body.

The baby wouldn't budge. The grape-coloured newborn was stuck in the birth canal.

"This baby must be huge," I said. "We'll never get it out."

"Crack its clavicle, Dokta."

"What?"

Sister's face remained surprisingly serene. "Fracture its collar bone so the shoulder will collapse inwards."

"Are you serious?"

"Yes. But no longer strong enough. Not with my arthritis. Feel for a clavicle and press two thumbs down." She demonstrated by placing her one thumb over the other and pretending to press down hard. "It should snap. Like a chicken bone."

I shuddered, then slid my fingers down the base of the baby's neck and felt for a clavicle. I felt a bone near the chest. Was it a rib or a clavicle? I couldn't tell for sure.

Would the baby die if I fractured a rib instead of a collarbone? Would I puncture the lung or poke through the heart?

The woman's cries rang in my ears. Veronika's eyes bulged with horror.

Panic welled up inside me.

I pressed on the bone. Nothing happened. I pressed harder. Still nothing. I crossed my thumbs, locked my wrists, and forced all my weight onto my hands.

Snap! Yes, just like a chicken bone. Tingles of revulsion shot across the back of my neck.

The infant's chest folded inwards, as Sister had predicted.

As if released from its casing, the shoulder slid beneath the mother's pelvis.

The arms came next, then the belly, and finally the rump and legs. In my arms, the baby girl felt enormous.

Twice the weight of an ordinary newborn, and perfectly proportioned. But completely still and utterly silent. She couldn't breathe. I'd got her out, but I'd killed her. My heart turned to lead.

Sister sucked strings of mucus from the infant's nose and mouth, then, with bag and mask, pumped oxygen into the lungs. Nothing.

I went through the motions of clamping and cutting the cord. Sister sucked again, then pumped more frantically.

A cry exploded from the infant's mouth. She lifted her arms and clenched pudgy fists. Her body flashed from feeble mauve to sturdy pink – and I felt my heart straining to burst out of my chest.

A few minutes later I found a pitcher of lemonade in Sister Bettina's fridge and guzzled it gratefully.

Sister walked in a moment later, smiling broadly. "You know how much that baby weighed?" She licked her lips at the sight of the lemonade. "Six kilos, two hundred grams. More than thirteen pounds."

"Wow!" I said in astonishment. "I've never seen a newborn over 10 pounds. No wonder she got stuck. How's her arm?"

"You saw for yourself. It's fine. No need to worry."

Sister was right. I'd seen the arm move well and the hand clench tightly in a fist. No nerve damage. Just a bruise over the collarbone.

With a figure-of-eight bandage tied across her chest and shoulders, the baby had seemed quite comfortable. The bone would quickly heal itself.

Lucy, one of the aides from the children's ward, approached with shy shuffles and watched me pour the frosty contents of a third tumbler down my throat.

"Excuse me, Dokta." She covered her gleaming buckteeth with her hand. "Edwina says please join us for a ward round."

Lucy slipped off and I followed a few minutes later.

We started in the back room of the ward, with the surgical

cases. I joked with Gervas, still a prisoner of the orthopedic traction I'd tethered to his leg some weeks before. The ten year-old had fallen from the top of the coconut tree he'd climbed in search of *kulaus*, the unripe nuts that hold nectar as clear and cool as spring water. He'd scraped his belly on the way down, and fractured his femur.

"We'll repeat the X-ray, Edwina," I said. "Today or tomorrow. We'll see how much healing there's been so far."

I rolled my eyes and held up two crossed fingers.

The day they'd carried Gervas into the hospital from the back of a truck, I'd shown his X-ray to his parents. The black-and-white image of the boy's thighbone looked like a stick of wood, a branch of frangipani, snapped in two. The parents screeched in horror.

Tears flooded the mother's face. The boy's face too. The father grabbed the X-ray and bashed his fist against the wall.

Their reactions puzzled me until the following day when the nurses explained the parents were convinced such a broken bone could never heal – their only son would never walk again, he'd be a hopeless cripple.

In response, I showed them the long scars where my own lower tibia was once fractured before being successfully repaired with screws.

"*Leg belong Dokta he been bagarup, all-same Gervas,*" I said. "*Now he goodpela.*" My healthy smile and normal gait had soon dried their tears.

I next reviewed some new admissions: Sepina with meningitis responding well to antibiotics; Anto whose spine was hunched and swollen with tuberculosis; and Freedah suffering her umpteenth episode of rheumatic fever.

Heart murmurs boomed so loudly across Freedah's skinny chest that I almost didn't need to take the stethoscope out of my satchel.

As always, the bloated bellies and skinny limbs of starving toddlers punctuated the in-patient landscape.

I noticed that none of the gaunt faces in need of our kwashiorkor-fighting formula had feeding tubes taped to their cheeks. I was puzzled for an instant before surmising the situation: It seemed the nurses had perfected the cup-and-spoon technique. They'd learned to coax the kids to swallow all their doses of VSF. Good for them – less fuss without the feeding tubes. Or so I thought.

As my initial uneasy feeling began to fade, I silently chided myself for being so surprised at the nurses' apparent initiative. Their skill at providing VSF would surely account for the missing feeding tubes.

But something else was missing: the smell of milk gone sour. Left in the bottom of a mug or dribbled onto a bed sheet, the VSF went off quickly in the heat.

Had the nurses marked my homecoming by scrupulously cleaning my favourite ward? That seemed unlikely.

My uneasy feeling returned.

I looked around. There were no mugs. No spoons, either. I flipped through the chart of a scrawny child: no doses of VSF logged neatly into the bedside notes.

"Where are the mugs of VSF, Edwina?"

No answer.

"Did Sister Leora run low on supplies while I was away?"

"No, Dokta," she replied, her eyes downcast.

"You *have* been giving the formula to the kids with kwashiorkor, eh?" My voice was thick with nervous tension.

Edwina batted a fly buzzing near her nose. "No."

I couldn't believe what I was hearing. The VSF had made this a happy ward. We'd brought Nalla's starving twins back to life. We'd seen them break out of their misery, then grow and flourish.

And we saw the same miracle every week – beaming mothers leaving the hospital with fat happy children, children who'd arrived only days before looking like living skeletons.

My cheeks, my ears, my throat flared like fireworks. "But... But why not?"

"The dokta didn't order it."

"But Edwina, you don't need a doctor to order the VSF. Your nurses always start the VSF on their own, whenever they diagnose a child with malnutrition."

"Yes, Dokta." She sighed and looked out the window, to some place far away, it seemed.

"Did Doctor Rudd tell you *not* to use the VSF?"

"No."

A hard claw of nausea gripped my stomach. "I don't understand… why did you stop?"

"Sister Pirmina said to wait for the new dokta to order it."

"And did he?"

"No."

That single word tore at my mind. Part of my soul went into every batch of VSF.

I'd thought Edwina thought the same way. But her face was as passive as a coconut husk. I could have coped if she'd shown she shared my disappointment, if she'd admitted they were wrong to stop giving the VSF. But her eyes reflected only empty indifference.

I erupted in rage and frustration: "You didn't bloody well bother to see those kids got the treatment they needed!"

Edwina looked away.

What a fool I'd been. I'd tricked myself into thinking this was my home. I didn't belong here; neither did my medical skills. Despite many, many hours of caring for patients, I was still nothing more than an outsider.

"Well that does it," I snapped. "You can finish the damn rounds on your own."

I wanted to bash my fist against the wall, but I felt too sick. Stomach-sick and heart-sick. I could see that at the end of my posting, when I moved on from Vunapope, everything I'd built, every program I'd nurtured, would crumble in my absence.

I ran from the ward and raced to my bungalow, where I threw myself on the bed and beat the pillow with my fists.

Sometime later, after the sun had set, the telephone rang a

relentless summons into the dark. I let it ring, again and again...

I counted fifteen rings then snatched the receiver from the bedside table.

"Yeah. What do you want?"

"Dokta... Dokta," said a female voice. "Please come to Men's Ward. A man with jaundice and abdominal pain."

"Call Doctor Rudd. Tell *him* to see the patient."

"But Dokta..."

I slammed down the phone and pulled the sheets over my head. When the phone rang again, I jammed the receiver under two pillows. I stumbled out of bed towards the bathroom and stubbed my toe on my suitcase. Dammit that hurt. Tears stung my eyes as I limped into the shower and shivered under the warm water.

I kept the telephone stifled under the pillows all the next day.

When voices called through the louvers and knuckles rapped on the doorframes, I crouched behind the bed.

"Leave me alone" was my only answer. There was nothing else to say. And too much more.

My suitcase, still packed with dirty clothes and souvenirs, taunted me: *We're done here, Buddy. No point in staying. This Development stuff is a waste of time. Let's take off, find ourselves a different adventure.*

Time passed slowly. After a day and a half without eating, I was ravenous. All I could find for breakfast: a tin of baked beans and a box of ant-infested crackers. I ate the beans straight from the can and cursed myself for letting the supply of groceries get so low.

The stack of aerograms, newly opened and scattered on the table, should have evoked a happy greeting at the end of my vacation; familiar handwriting on an envelope always made me feel aglow.

But now, peeling back these flimsy flaps was a chore, and reading the chatty missives as pleasurable as shovelling snow.

I found the cheery details of my cousin's birthday party a petty waste of postage.

The unexpected phrases blurted from the mouths of "gifted"

toddlers, quoted verbatim by their parents, made me groan.

Footsteps shuffled outside the kitchen door. "Dokta! Father Schiermann here."

"And Sister Leora," chirped a female voice.

"Are you all right, Dokta?" Father Schiermann asked. "Everyone is worried about you."

He did sound worried in a friendly sort of way. I mumbled a half-hearted reply: "I'm okay, I guess."

I didn't get up from my chair. They could say their piece through the louvers.

"Sister Pirmina wanted to break down your door with an axe," Sister Leora said, "but I hoped an apple strudel would do the trick. Sister Assumpta's famous recipe."

"A terrible thing must be wrong," Father said. "Can we make it right?"

"We need you," said Sister. "Not just your medical skills, but your friendship, too."

"And inspiration," said Father, peering through the mosquito mesh of the screen window.

They were laying it on a bit thick. Yeah, sure I provided inspiration. So much inspiration that everything fell apart as soon as I turned my back.

I looked about the kitchen – a few dirty glasses by the sink and a couple of crushed cockroaches on the floor.

Pushing myself up from the table, I basked in the rancid sweat soaking the shirt and shorts I'd worn for a day and two nights, and kicked the cockroach carcasses more or less beneath the refrigerator.

"Hi," I grunted to the earnest pair standing on my doorstep.

"Oh Dokta," said Sister Leora, holding up the strudel. "I'm so glad to see you're all right."

"So am I," Father Schiermann said. He glanced at the strudel, at his feet, at the rip in my tee-shirt sleeve He cleared his throat, covering his mouth with a fist. "Sister Pirmina heard from the nurses that you were very upset in the children's ward."

I lifted the pan of strudel from Sister Leora's crooked fingers.

"I guess you want to come in?"

Sister shook her head. Her eyes fluttered behind her spectacles. "I must get back to the pharmacy. But maybe Father..."

"Yes," Father interrupted. "But I won't stay long."

We sat at the kitchen table.

Father refused offers of coffee and strudel. He placed his hands flat on the table – no rings or rosary, just callused fingers, marked by physical labour, that presented the communion host every day of the year.

The aerograms caught Father's eye. "Did you get bad news from home?"

"No. Nothing like that."

"Would you like to tell me what has upset you? They tell me you haven't your phone or your door answered for two days."

I responded to his question with one of my own: "Have you been to the children's ward lately?"

"No," he said, shaking his head. "Why? Is something wrong going on there?"

I slammed the tin of beans against the tabletop. "It's what's *not* going on that's the problem."

Father looked puzzled.

"Our VSF program," I snapped. "The nurses abandoned it while I was away. Let kids starve just like before. Let them lie there till they died."

My face was on fire, my throat dry as Arctic air, and my cheeks soaked with the tears I couldn't hold back. "Edwina knew exactly what to do but she didn't bloody bother. I go off on a few days' holiday and the VSF program dies. So what's the point of being here?"

I wanted to say more but my frustration, my rage, rendered me speechless. My life here had truly lost all meaning. My work, my contribution, had all the permanence of footprints on the beach, a brief impression washed away by the unforgiving tides. There was no appreciation or value accorded my work, only soul-destroying indifference. And I could take no more of it.

15

Bita Paka

Twenty minutes after my outburst in my kitchen, I was seated beside Father Schiermann in his Land Cruiser as we drove along a winding road.

Father had insisted on taking me on a long drive to a place called Bita Paka. And I, with considerable reluctance, had agreed to be his passenger.

As we drove along, I stared silently at the sea through the strobe-like flicker of sunlight between the coconut trunks hugging the roadside.

Father gripped the steering wheel of his Land Cruiser with his right hand and thrust his left into a bag of candy.

"We'll be there in a few minutes only," he said. "Help yourself to a sweet. I prefer chocolate, but peppermints are not melting into a big mess."

Taking a candy, I stared at the wrapper's foreign language.

"My sister sends them from Germany," he said. "Every Christmas enough peppermint to last one year. She worries about me. Wonders how I manage without beer, German chocolate, and bratwurst."

He swerved to avoid a clump of coconut fronds littering the road. "At least she doesn't send sausages in the post."

A hot peppery menthol exploded on my tongue. "Are you going to tell me about this Bita Paka place, Father?"

He shook his head. "It's better you see it the first time without advance preparation."

Father turned onto a dirt track that led through a thicket of cocoa and banana trees. A small white sign of battered tin stated: *Bita Paka 2 km*. He glanced over at me: "You'll see what I mean."

The jeep pitched and banged over potholes. Rocks rattled the floor. Branches scraped the sides. Where were we going?

When I'd tearfully erupted at my kitchen table, Father stood, rattled his car keys, and said: "Have you been ever to Bita Paka?"

"No. What is it?"

"I call it my *Gedenkschlupfwinkel*. I don't know the English word for it. My special den for remembering, perhaps. Put on a clean shirt. We go there now." Moments later we were on the road.

The track drew us into an opening in the forest and terminated at a parking lot.

We climbed out of the vehicle and onto a walkway, lined by giant clamshells. It led us to a clearing dominated by a wrought iron arch.

Large black letters stated: *BITA PAKA WAR CEMETERY.* Smaller letters underneath proclaimed: *Commonwealth War Graves Commission.*

Beyond the archway, rows of low white cubes charted a matrix on manicured lawn. The massive scale, the noiseless dignity, the geometrical perfection riveted my feet to the stony pavement.

Father stepped through the archway. "Come. It is permitted to walk inside."

I tucked in my shirt, and followed Father to the first row of white stone markers. Two generous paces of closely clipped lawn separated each grave from its neighbours.

A bronze plaque capped every pedestal with a name, a division, and a 1940s date of death.

I strolled along the rows and read the names – William, Stephen, Harold, James…

A mynah bird flitted ahead of me, from one marker to the next and squawked cheekily.

Shivers rocked my frame when I imagined the hundreds of youthful corpses beneath our feet.

"A thousand young men are buried here," said Father. "The names of twelve hundred more, missing in action, are engraved on those tablets over there." He pointed to an avenue of stone pylons.

"Coming here reminds me that these men gave their lives so one day a priest like me… a German priest, could bring our Lord's message of peace and goodwill to New Britain."

Father scuffed the turf. "Our lives are short. When we have the chance, we must burn bright."

He looked at me and held my gaze. "For every patient you look after, Dokta, you are a lantern in a dark land."

My ears burned. I turned and stared at the avenue of tall memorial monoliths.

Each line of engraving cradled a young man – nearly all even younger than me – forever lost and far from home.

Father cleared his throat. "Like the battles won or lost by the soldiers, our struggles can seem hopeless. Our successes only temporary. But we do touch people's lives in ways that last forever. Look at Nalla's malnourished twins. They are healthy still, and every day chasing their mother's chickens."

I smiled at the thought of Simon's hugs and the warmth of his fevered chest against mine. CUSO mavens put little importance on the present; they lauded master plans, long-term goals, and legacies. But perhaps they had it wrong.

There *was* magic in every moment, even if those moments didn't last.

Until the last day of my Vunapope posting, my VSF would make a difference to every kid who took it. After that, both the malnutrition treatment program and the future would have to take care of themselves. No regrets. Well, yes, I would have regrets, but not so many wasted tears.

On the drive back, I felt embarrassed about returning to the hospital. I'd been dismayed for the children who wouldn't get my VSF once I'd left. But also I'd been sulking because no one appreciated the great legacy I thought I'd be leaving behind.

Surely the hospital would be abuzz over my outburst and my two days in seclusion.

Should I tell them I'd been sick? But with what? Sister Pirmina would never believe it. She'd enjoy my discomfort, and I cringed at the thought of seeing her.

As we pulled up the driveway to the reception area, Sister Bettina suddenly appeared, running towards us.

She waved her arms and scurried towards my side of the vehicle. "Dokta. Mrs. Dawna is in the private ward. Arrived an hour ago with abdominal pain and rapid pulse. The pain is quite severe. Sister Pirmina says it's only gastro. But I think it's serious."

Damn! I knew she should have gone back to Canada to have the baby. I felt like throwing up. "When is the baby due?"

"Not for another eight weeks."

Now I had three patients to contend with: Dawna; her premature fetus; and, Garnet, likely filled with guilt and anxiety.

Stomach churning, I headed for the private ward and prayed Sister Pirmina was correct; that Dawna had nothing more serious than gastroenteritis.

But the lessons of Bita Paka burned in my mind. Whatever the challenge, I knew I would face it. And win.

My gait quickened and my spirit grew stronger as I walked towards Dawna's bedside. My confidence was restored.

I was again ready and willing to provide my patient with whatever medical care she needed...

Epilogue:
My Son Shares His Story

My dad said I should write this part of his book since I was there when it happened and he wasn't.

It was years ago but it's taken that long for me to be able to talk about it. I was fourteen, in my first year of high school. I tried out for the school band and they let me join as second drummer. I prefer jamming in our basement with my friends who play electric guitar, but Mum said it would be "good discipline" to play in the school band. I auditioned, thinking I was just a puny grade niner and there was no way they'd take me.

But the music teacher said I was good at keeping rhythm and gave me my acceptance in a letter that said I had an "innate sense of timing," whatever that means. My mum saw the envelope tucked into my math homework, so after that I just had to join the band.

It wasn't so bad, really. We got maroon jackets that named our high school band on the back and had our names on the sleeve. Some parents made a fuss about putting our names on the jackets where anyone could read them and maybe take advantage of us. The principal got involved, then the school board trustees.

Finally, they let us kids choose whether we wanted our first or last name, or no name at all on our own jacket. I went with first and last. Like, was I really going to be kidnapped or molested because a stranger could read my name on the sleeve of my band jacket?

We went to Winnipeg, Manitoba in mid-December for a school-band jamboree with twenty bands from all over Canada. Between rehearsals, me and a couple of friends went shopping downtown.

What a cold place Winnipeg is. The stores are connected by underground tunnels to protect people from the freezing wind. I bought a pack of gum but didn't see anything else I wanted.

We thought we'd head back to a pizza place we'd passed on another street, so we took an escalator up towards an exit.

My friends, Roddy and Tyler, rode a couple of steps ahead of me, and a lady stood beside me. She was about my parents' age and was holding two Sony Store shopping bags.

When we got to street level, Roddy and Tyler slid through the exit door ahead of me. The wind blew the door closed with a loud crash but the guys didn't seem to notice.

I pushed the heavy door open again and held it so the lady could walk through. She gave me a big smile and said: "thank you, young man." She looked at my name on my band jacket. "Your father is a doctor, isn't he? A paediatrician."

I wanted to say I didn't know any doctors, and then run and catch my friends, who were heading along the crowded sidewalk to the next corner. But the woman had stopped right in the doorway and I couldn't just let the door go and have it crash into her.

"Yes," I said, hoping that would be the end of it, but knowing it wouldn't be. Anyone who's known my dad since he was young says the same thing: "You look and sound exactly like your father. What an amazing resemblance."

I can't see it. We both ski and scuba dive, but Dad's got white hair and a grey moustache. He looks after sick people and teaches medical students at the university.

The lady just stood there, holding her bags, smiling, and blocking the doorway. "Your dad just *must* be Ross Pennie."

"That's right." I wanted to end the conversation but she had such a big smile I couldn't help looking at her face.

"He saved my life, you know. In Papua New Guinea. Did you know he was a doctor there?"

"Yup." Roddy and Tyler were now way down the sidewalk.

"I had complications when my first was born. Your dad delivered him by Caesarean section before we both bled to death."

For a moment, she didn't say anything – remembering I guess. Then she gave a big smile.

"I think of your dad every Christmas when my family gets together. Nick was two months premature. Now he's 24, and six-foot-two. He's got his pilot's license and wants to fly jets some day. Garnet and I also have two other kids, 21 and 19."

The lady stopped to take a breath and realized she was blocking the doorway. She stepped outside. I could barely see my friends crossing the street at the intersection. They'd soon be out of sight.

The lady put her bags down on the sidewalk. "Sorry. I should introduce myself, eh?" She held out her hand, it was covered by a mitten. "I'm Dawna Wallis. I live up in..."

There was a sudden screech of tires and the sound of cars smashing into each other. I'd never seen a car crash up close before. I ran towards it. Black smoke billowed up from the hood of a delivery van. It had tipped over on two wheels and leaned against a department store. The driver was slumped over his steering wheel, his face covered in blood. A huge display window was totally smashed, and plastic elves, a team of wooden reindeer, and mounds of fake snow were spilled all over the sidewalk.

It was weird. The traffic completely stopped. Then I saw two bodies, face down in the middle of the intersection. You couldn't miss the big white letters on the backs of their jackets identifying our high school.

I don't remember much about the funeral for Roddy and Tyler. Everyone was crying.

I couldn't keep my eyes off the two coffins. The minister made a speech and said something about the guys being in the wrong place at the wrong time. That made me feel so weird that when the service was over, I couldn't budge from my spot. I kept thinking about that lady in Winnipeg, and how she delayed me or I could have been killed as well.

Thanks to her, I was in the right place at the right time.

I also thought about how she and her baby nearly died. But they didn't. And now her son's a pilot.

When my dad squeezed my arm and guided me out of the church, I realized that a long time ago, way before I was born, he'd also been in the right place at the right time.

Editor's Note:

We hope you've enjoyed Dr. Pennie's *The Unforgiving Tides*, relating the author's experiences as a CUSO volunteer physician.
For more information on CUSO, visit the organization's Web site: www.cuso.org or email: cuso.secretariat@cuso.ca
CUSO toll-free: 1-888-434-2876.   Fax: 613-829-7996.
Mail: CUSO, 500-2255 Carling Ave, Ottawa, ON, K2B 1A6

Manor House Publishing
www.manor-house.biz
(905) 648-219